More Manchester than Mongolia

An Unexpected Road Trip Through Back Road Britain

Jacqueline Lambert

World Wide Walkies

ISBN (ebook): 978-1-7396222-4-4
ISBN (paperback): 978-1-7396222-5-1

Cover design by Linn Hart and Paul Hawkins (BolderBooks.com)

Formatting by Atticus

Dedication

To Sue, my bestie since school, on your marriage to Stuart: 12th September 2025.

Though we were off roaming in The Beast and couldn't be there, we wish you every happiness for the road ahead – and I'm glad that reading my books hasn't put you off your own campervan dreams!

Contents

More Manchester Than Mongolia

An Unexpected Road Trip Through Back Road Britain

MONGOLIA
10000 miles

SCOTLAND

Where we got married!

Glasgow & NC500 - keep going!

MANCHESTER

Ingleton

KEY

Waddington

Preston   In the grip of a tyre fitters hand...

HB

Blackburn
Hometown

HB - Hebden Bridge

MANCHESTER

Marple

Mappleton

Grantham

KEY

Corby

JB Rubber

KEY

Shooting Box

Bosworth

Stratford-upon-Avon

Ironbridge

Crouch

Coventry

Walton-in-Fens

Rutland

Malmesbury

WALES

Overland Show

ENGLAND

Vet

Mystery Location!
Sinkhole:
Tiles:
Sorted

Tyger!

Oxford

Wantage

London

Winchester

Bournemouth
Home Base

N

Map Not To Scale
& Unsuitable for Navigation!

Chapter 1

Prologue

In 2016, my husband, Mark, and I created a monster.

Not a mechanical one – that would come later – but something more subtle and far more disruptive: an inability to settle in one place.

'About a month' is a timeline that looms large in our lives.

Mark proposed to me 37 days after we met. (We were married after 37 weeks.)

We acquired our pack, The Fab Four, in a similar whirlwind fashion.

The plan was to get two Cavapoos (Cavalier King Charles Spaniel/Poodle cross) to keep each other company. But a fortnight and a half later we had three. First came our black-and-white babies, Kai and Rosie, a boy and a girl. But when we collected Rosie, the breeder unveiled a litter of russet-coloured pups, and we fell in love. After a week of trying to be sensible and talk Mark out of it, a foxy-red princess, Ruby, trotted into our lives.

Three, however, is not a good number, so naturally we completed the set of cuddly, teddy-bear-faced pooches with our tiny black minx, Lani.

Our decision to travel full-time came when we were made redundant five years too soon. Staring down the barrel of 'what now?' and worrying how we'd stay afloat financially, we went out one day *just to look* – and accidentally bought a caravan.

Celebrating our purchase begat a tipsy proposal: if we rented out our flat and hit the road, maybe we would never have to work again...

Once sober, it took us a month to sell our stuff and go.

It was supposed to be a three-year trip. Sufficient to purge the wanderlust from our systems.

But we never quite stopped... until Brexit slammed the brakes on our dream of endless European travel.

Limited to stays no longer than 90 days in every 180 in most of Europe, we did what any sensible couple would do.

Within a month, we'd purchased a 24.5-tonne ex-army truck – blind off the internet – to escape the shackles of Schengen and drive to Mongolia.

The chaos, comedy, and catastrophe of turning that truck – The Beast – into a functioning home is the subject of my previous book, *Building The Beast: How (Not) To Build an Overland Camper*.

This is the story of what happened next.

Chapter 2

Volvo Means I Roll - Straight into Chaos!

F inally, after the second coronavirus lockdown trapped Mark and me 'in the brick' for eight months, we were back on the road.

'The brick' in question was a compact but characterful apartment set in beautiful grounds. Once, we believed it would be our forever home. But we'd rented it out – then sold it – to fund a crazy mission.

Caravan Kismet, our sanctuary and faithful travel companion for the previous five years, was also gone. Instead, we were in The Beast, a 1990 Volvo N10 expedition truck we'd bought from the Belgian army.

The Beast was our first DIY conversion. A lumbering off-grid fortress we'd coaxed into being with stubborn optimism – and a lot of help from friends.

The project went entirely to plan. In fact, we finished the work early, which allowed us a couple of weeks to test all the systems and ensure everything was working perfectly before we set off.

Who am I kidding?

This is Lambertshire.

Nothing would ever go that smoothly with a brace of truckin' idiots in charge!

***

Volvo means 'I roll'.

It comes from the Latin verb *volvere* – to turn, revolve, keep moving... A Swedish ball bearing company figured it packed more marketing zing than *Jag rullar,* which is how they roll in Gothenburg.

Yet for many months, even with six wheels on my wagon, the only thing still rolling along was time...

The Beast should have been ready.

That was the plan.

Miles, the chap who helped us convert the truck, was a talented but commitment-phobic artisan. When we delivered his blank, six-wheeled canvas in February, we said we needed it complete by October, ready for our departure to Mongolia. He took in the square lines of our unregistered, bull-nosed truck and promised, "I'll have that done by July!"

But this was not destined to be a Midsummer Night's Dream.

Shakespeare's Lysander might easily have said to Hermia, "The course of truck conversion ne'er did run smooth..."

And as we'd discovered through five years of Adventure Caravanning, a plan is merely a comedy script, sketched in pencil.

Eighteen months after Miles made his faithful pledge of a five-month turnaround, we found ourselves trying to draw the final curtain on a build that had seen more false dawns than a dodgy soap opera. A global coronavirus pandemic, then Brexit, added unforeseen complications to the fact that our crew often vanished more swiftly than socks in a launderette.

Based on Miles' solid assurances that The Beast would be ready, we'd sold both the caravan and our flat the previous October to pay for the build.

But to Miles, it seemed, deadlines were aspirational. Like mirages in the desert, they shimmered tantalisingly on the horizon, only to vanish the second you got close.

When October arrived, the truck had no windows, door, roof lights, plumbing, LPG gas system, lighting, or even a framework for the interior furnishings.

Which forced us to rent our flat back from its new owners!

Months later, on Miles' confident assertion that he would definitely finish The Beast by the end of the following June, we'd given our landlords notice.

So, in mid-June, when he went AWOL and left us with a still unfinished truck, he landed us in a peculiar bind.

We couldn't stay in our home, and we couldn't rent anywhere either. It seems that in real-estate-speak, 'We have four small, well-behaved, non-shedding dogs' translates directly as, 'Dealbreaker: Code RED.'

This upped the stakes somewhat.

Every setback, every delay, pushed us closer to the edge. The Beast wasn't finished. But as the 30th of June approached, we no longer had the luxury to postpone.

***

When D-Day (Departure Day) finally arrived, by midday, we should have been rolling on a leisurely cruise towards the Self Build Campervan Get Together in Wantage, Oxfordshire. Then later, maybe even raising a well-deserved glass to our new beginning. To the Grand Design we'd been through hell to bring to fruition.

Besides meeting up with Alex, the electrician who'd rescued us in our darkest hour when our sparkie and plumber, Iain, had also walked off the job, we had perverse logic in making this our first stop.

In the back of my mind lurked the conviction that if any problems arose on our maiden voyage, someone would know what to clout with a hammer. Alex had also sweetened the deal with top-secret intel: a TV crew filming for *Million Pound Motorhomes* wanted to look at The Beast.

Yet, instead of rolling up the A34 to Wantage, at 8:30 p.m., we were still in Bournemouth, working flat-out on the truck.

A tenant was already installed in our former forever home, so we were officially homeless.

Ready or not, we had only one option.

To move into The Beast.

***

Ever the optimist, I had said to Mark, "It doesn't matter if we haven't completed the cosmetics, so long as we have the basics: electricity, gas, and water."

Well, we had electricity.

The water pump wouldn't work, and a strong whiff of gas lurked menacingly under the hob.

Henry, our emergency stand-in plumber, had a full-time job, so the leaks would have to wait. I filled every container I could find with water, turned off the gas at the cylinder, and made a mental note to sleep with the windows open. And maybe not wander around like Wee Willie Winkie wafting candles, blowtorches, or practising fire eating. Then, I steeled myself to endure the trauma of coping with all this stress with no tea or coffee.

Fortunately, unlike the terrible day five years before when we left late to embark on our new life of full-time touring in Caravan Kismet, we had wine.

Never let it be said that experience has taught us nothing!

Had Marie Antoinette faced spending a night in the back of a truck without plumbing, I bet she'd have ditched the cake and proclaimed, "If they don't have water, let them drink wine."

***

We had wine, but no plan B.

The rules at Miles' yard, the Vision Vault, prohibited overnight stays.

Out of options, I stood beside our unfinished truck, dangerously close to tears. Not a feeling you expect on the first day of the rest of your life. It was rather reminiscent of our first night in Caravan Kismet when, following a near death experience on the road, we found ourselves living the dream late at night with no food (or wine), in a caravan that stunk of fox poo because four hysterical puppies decided that was a foolproof way to adjust to their new circumstances.

People often ask why we called our truck The Beast. The answer is simple. She is HUGE! 33 ft long, 12.6 ft high, and 8.4 ft wide (10 x 3.85 x 2.55 m). Although she is 24.5 tonnes gross, fully converted, we estimated she sat at around 15 tonnes.

She has a top speed of 45 mph (72 kph), which already spelled a midnight arrival at our intended stopover – an unknown field 80 miles (129 km) away, somewhere in the wilds near Wantage.

It was our maiden voyage. First time out, the idea of threading our oversized lump of Swedish steel through pitch-black country lanes filled us with just about infinite terror.

Yet, there we were in Bournemouth, with no clue where to park a vehicle the size of a small castle.

In our cosseted caravan days, we'd always stayed on official camp-sites. Kismet was not cut out for life off-grid. She needed water on tap and an electrical hook-up. Camping off-grid was the whole point of The Beast – we simply had no clue how to go about it.

A long-term van lifer, Miles took pity and guided us to one of his secret countryside park-ups. After medicating ourselves with fermented grape juice and draping dog blankets over the windows because we had no blinds, we collapsed into bed, utterly spent.

The following morning, Miles fixed the gas leak and around lunchtime, we set off to the Self Build Get Together. A day-and-a-half late: eight months behind our planned October departure – or a mere year behind schedule, counting from the initial July deadline Miles had promised.

We'd missed the first night's fun, along with our shot at stardom on the Channel 5 documentary *Million Pound Motorhomes*, but at least we were finally on a roll.

***

The truck wasn't ready. We weren't ready. But here's the thing about blindly chasing a dream. There's never a perfect moment. Only a series of wildly imperfect ones – and if you wait until everything's ready, you might never leave.

So we left.

For the first time, I sat in the cab with Mark. The Beast's engine roared into life, and we rumbled into the sunset.

Volvo means *I roll*.

Not, *I wait until the stars align*, or, *I cry like a baby and give up*. Just *I roll*.

Ready or not.

Straight into our next adventure.

And the kind of chaos that could only happen to a pair of truckin' idiots.

Chapter 3

Wanted in Wantage

If an alien landed in Britain and demanded the lowdown on British country roads, I would offer them this short acclimatisation speech.

"Hi! Yes. Welcome to Britain! You just touched down.

"What was that? You want to learn about local infrastructure? No problem. I'm the perfect person to ask! Because we've got to drive this huge truck on it. No. Not on a motorway. Onto... Well. I think it's a road. At least, that's what it says on the map...

"So. British country roads. Let me explain.

"I'm not sure how things are where you're from, but I'm guessing you are picturing 'roads' as wide, paved corridors, designed for smooth, efficient transport. Yes? Oh, that's adorable. But it's not how things are here....

"In the British countryside, we prefer something a little more... intimate.

"Can you visualise a 'lane'?

"Yes. It's narrow.

"Nope. Narrower than that.

"Here. Let me paint a picture. It's narrower than a greyhound lying down. No. A greyhound lying down *lengthways*.

"Now *squeeeeze* in a hedge on both sides. No. Not beside the road. In the road. Yes – a tall one. Tall enough to blot out the sun.

"Of course there are trees that lean in. I mean, the council does its best to chop off the branches to a height of four metres, but there's not much they can do if the trunk isn't straight or has a burr or growth on it. If you're driving a high vehicle, as well as looking ahead, you must look out above, to the sides – and drive down the middle of the road to avoid them.

"No, you're right. It's not always hedges and trees that blot out the sun. It could be a bank with a dry-stone wall on top. And sometimes there are ditches. Yes – deep ones. Certainly. They could easily swallow an asteroid!

"What? You think a narrow road with obstacles on each side must be one way? Oh, goodness me. No! It's designed for two-way traffic!

"Well, of course it's not straight. That would be boring! Imagine a snake having a seizure. Yes. They're *that* bendy. And the trees, hedges, walls, and narrowness mean that most of the bends are completely blind.

"And then there's the road surface. You'd think, wouldn't you?! Do you remember when you passed the moon? It's a bit like that. There are potholes and craters, but it's also slick with mud, manure, and the entrails of dead badgers. The manure? Mostly from all the horses, cows, and other unexpected livestock you'll find wandering around on there. Sometimes, when you turn a corner, there's an entire flock of sheep!

"No, it's not only animals. There are walkers, cyclists. Perhaps an occasional combine harvester!

"What? Streetlights? In the hours of darkness? Don't be silly! It's the countryside. That would ruin the ambience.

"Of course you can't see what's coming! Not even in daylight – it's so narrow and bendy! Out here, we navigate with nothing more than the faint glow of our own panic reflecting off damp brambles. You simply learn to *sense* it.

"Reversing? Naturally. That happens a lot. Up hills. Around bends. Usually under the silent judgement of a country pub's full beer garden...

"Road signs? Well, occasionally, you'll see one that says, 'Beware. Oncoming Vehicles in Middle of Road'. It's nice. It's comforting, but it's unnecessary. I mean. That's how it is all the time!

"The speed limit? Well, that's the best part. It's sixty miles an hour. No. Not six-*teen*. Sixty. Six-zero. Happily, it's in lovely, Imperial miles per hour. It would scare you to death in metric. In km / h, it's 96.5!

"But the speed limit is irrelevant if you're local. Then, you simply go as fast as you can thrash a beaten-up Peugeot 305 with ten people inside, while smoking a fag on your way back from the pub.

"Anyway. I must get going. Side mirrors folded. Left wing in a hedge. Right wing in someone's rhododendrons. Crikey! That pheasant just screamed at me. And there's a tractor half the width of the planet approaching. We're left-hand drive, you know. We need to suck in our shoulders and question our life choices...

"My advice to you?

"Perhaps you and your spaceship should stick to the M4..."

***

As you may surmise, British country roads are not the most confidence-inspiring terrain on which to debut a ten-metre, 24.5-tonne gross, left-hand drive truck.

Driving The Beast was a physical challenge. Steering demanded the sort of upper-body strength normally exhibited by champion weightlifters or those rare souls capable of opening a stubborn pickle jar. Every gear change required a distance of travel akin to the Herculean sweep of an Olympic medal-winning oarsman.

I began to understand why Mark, who likes to live dangerously, had once ventured tentatively, "I don't think you'll be able to drive The Beast."

Back then, in a froth of feminist fury, I'd growled, "I can fly a frikkin' plane, Mark. I can drive a truck."

But The Beast is not just any truck. It's more Lancaster Bomber than Cessna 150 – and with the driver's seat lowered fully, my feet still didn't reach the floor!

Even from the passenger seat, my role in The Beast's safe conduct was anything but passive. I assumed the mantle co-pilot, issuing a running commentary on the road ahead. Knobbly off-road tyres and a suspension with the subtlety of a kangaroo strapped to a trampoline with bungee cords made each bump an airborne adventure. Gear changes forced me to engage my core as they flung me backwards and forwards like a rag doll. Each assault forcibly expelled my breath, adding a rather strange emphasis to my navigational announcements.

"Low br-ANCH left. Tight BEND fif-TY YARDS. Cy-CLIST approa-CHING. PED-estrian left. Large VEH-icle a-HEAD."

Twenty miles in, we pulled into a service station, exhausted. With little water and no gas, we were desperate for our first coffee of the day – and a chance to recalibrate emotionally.

There, we got a taste of what was to come.

The sort of reaction a unique one-off vehicle like The Beast provokes.

A lady in the car park asked to look inside.

Mid-afternoon, we rolled into the Self Build Campervan meet through a long avenue of trees. Our cab was so high, it rode through the canopy. Green branches obscured the windscreen, before the steel deflectors we'd fitted to the cab roof lifted them. They rustled and scuffed along our roofline, but didn't snag on the solar panels.

A small welcoming party gathered with cameras and phones. They filmed our arrival like a wildlife documentary crew capturing footage of an unknown species for the very first time. In the field sprawled a sea of voguish vans, upcycled ambulances, and bijou buses, festooned with awnings and fairy lights. Many sported graphics of mountains and nautical compasses to proclaim their adventurous intent and far-flung dreams. The Beast stood out like a prehistoric megalosaurus that had somehow lumbered into a petting zoo. Fifteen tonnes of matte-green menace crunched over the gravel as Mark reversed around a corner through a narrow gateway, with a decorative post placed inconveniently mid-arc. I closed my eyes as our audience held their breath. Despite the pressure, Mark nailed it.

We swung down from the cab with a slight air of seasoned long-haul truckers, although our wafer-thin cover of casual competence was about to be blown wide open.

Darren, Alex's fellow organiser, came by to welcome us, eyes twinkling with admiration.

"Nice rig!" he said. "What make?"

"Volvo N10," Mark replied.

"How old?"

"30 years."

"Engine size?"

"9.6 litres."

"Straight six or V6?"

Mark hesitated, before taking a wild punt. "Errr, straight..." he uttered, with all the conviction of a man grappling blindly in a 'guess the weight of the marrow' competition at a village fête.

Darren's final question was so obscure and technical, I can't remember what it was. Mark blinked, then answered, "Now, you've lost me..."

The next humiliation followed in short order when our heroic electrician, Alex, came to greet us.

"Glad you made it!" He grinned. When we told him our water pump wouldn't work, he popped inside and fixed it in seconds.

It was the fuse.

***

A steady stream of visitors came in to view The Beast, whose decor contrasted starkly with her utilitarian NATO green livery.

Inside, we'd cast subtlety aside and made a unique interior statement. In stark defiance against Caravan Kismet's tasteful, mass-produced beige-on-beige neutrality, we'd gone full, joy-inducing technicolour.

We'd leaned toward an underwater look. As obsessive-compulsive windsurfers, we couldn't resist letting our passion ripple through into The Beast's design.

The upper cupboards, in stained spruce ply, were sunburnt orange and yellow ochre. A gentle waft with a blowtorch before staining scorched the natural wood grain into shadowy relief. We'd upholstered our sofa in a vivid camouflage pattern of indigo, tangerine, and turquoise, which echoed the bright cupboards and paint-washed aquamarine walls. Even Mark had flinched at my choice of material, but I told him to trust me and be bold... The result was stupendous!

In our wet room, shimmering Perspex both varnished and water-proofed the spruce panels. They rose in a scorched and stained Tequila Sunrise gradient through all hues of marmalade, from dark Seville to glowing mandarin. Opposite, in the same warm fiery colours, we'd mounted a four-foot high (1.2 m) surfboard-shaped mirror – a thoughtful gift crafted for us by Miles, the kingpin of our build. In polished wood, it featured the lithe silhouette of a surf girl in the centre, stretching against her board.

The surf theme cropped up again in the colourful nose-end of a surfboard we'd repurposed as a partition between the kitchen and sofa. The worktop was the kitchen's dominant feature. A single slab of oiled, live-edge sequoia, whose heartwood gleamed like amber, fringed by pale gold sapwood.

At the back, next to the rear barn doors, which we could throw open to invite the outside in, our slightly larger-than-super-king-size bed sported a lively ocean-inspired royal blue and white duvet.

The moment they crossed the threshold, it was easy to tell who approved.

Most nodded with impressed admiration, while a few froze mid-step, their faces caught somewhere between disbelief and mild trauma.

We didn't mind. Ultimately, we'd created The Beast to please ourselves – such is the freedom and delight of a self-build. The outcome was not just a living space. It was an exuberant, unapologetic reflection of ourselves, and we adored every riotous, kaleidoscopic inch!

The Self Build Get Together is all about helping each other and sharing knowledge. We saw little of Alex – other than his legs poking out from beneath a succession of vans. Rather than working on his own vehicle, with tireless generosity, he valiantly spent his entire weekend fixing a plethora of problems for others. Truly, a knight in grimy armour!

We were pretty clueless, although we swiftly got used to fielding the same handful of questions. It didn't take long to spot a pattern, so we turned it into a running game: Lorry Life Bingo. Everyone wanted to know the same things about The Beast, so we entertained ourselves by predicting what might crop up next, and logging each query to our daily tally.

With a hulking truck and its near ten-litre engine, the initial approach is usually some variation of, "How many gallons to the mile does that do?!" or "I wouldn't want your fuel bills!"

To which we reply, "Ah, but I think you might!"

What the inquisitor always fails to grasp is that The Beast is not an expensive car: it's a cheap house. I enjoy watching the penny slowly drop as I explain, "Diesel is pretty much our only ongoing expense."

We designed The Beast to survive off-grid for weeks at a time. Solar panels, which cover almost the entire roof, generate 1300 watts of power from the sun. Sufficient to run any electrical gadget, and plenty to keep 720 amp hours of AGM (Absorbent Glass Mat) batteries charged. All green energy – and no electricity bills.

Two refillable 20-litre (5 gallon) LPG gas cylinders provided for all our cooking, heating, and hot water needs. We'd used them in the caravan, so we knew they lasted three months each and cost pennies to refill. After all, we only needed to heat the equivalent of a single small room, and took brief showers to conserve the 350 litres (77 gallons) of water we carried onboard.

Since we were self-sufficient and no longer needed to pay for a campsite every night – another big saving – we calculated that, compared to Caravan Kismet, it would take at least five years before The

Beast's higher fuel costs caught up with our previous budget.

Another classic Lorry Life Bingo remark came next: "That's a 'Go-Anywhere' truck. You must have been *everywhere* with that thing!" Mark and I exchanged glances.

Sheepishly, I admitted that our magnificent off-road vehicle had journeyed all the way from Bournemouth to Wantage.

Then, I had to confess that due to COVID restrictions, our plans for the foreseeable future were very much, "More Manchester than Mongolia."

***

For the time being, Mongolia was firmly on hold.

With coronavirus restrictions sealing the UK's borders, we couldn't even leave our own island. As a farewell gift, our friends Fiona and Mike had handed us a guide to the newly launched NC500 (North Coast 500) – a 516-mile route designed to lure tourists into the wild corners of Scotland's far north. Back then, it was more cult classic than the blockbuster it is today. Hardly anyone – ourselves included – had heard of it.

Looking back to my travels B.C. (Before Canines), I still can't believe I saw New Zealand before I set foot in Scotland.

When I first gazed upon the dramatic scenery in the Highlands and the Isle of Skye, I asked myself, *"How come I flew to the other side of the world when I've got THIS right on my doorstep?!"*

So often, we chase adventure in far-flung destinations and overlook the beauty in our backyard.

Britain is a compact marvel. After travelling on six continents, I can say truthfully that few places match its variety of landscapes, culture, and history, squeezed into such a small area.

I'd always been saving Britain and Western Europe for when I was too decrepit to grind across Kazakhstan.

But faced with no choice, I was excited at the prospect of exploring my home turf.

Conventional trip planning has never been our forte. Once, Mark and I organised an entire holiday around an umbrella museum mentioned in our Italian language textbook.

Mike and Fiona had supplied the blueprint, and we had a few jobs to do on the way north.

So, we settled on Scotland.

Chapter 4

The Iron Lady of Grantham - Overland Adventures in the UK!

O ne way to make things difficult for yourself is to use a UK postcode to find a park-up in a rural location, then try to drive there in a 24.5-tonne truck.

For those unfamiliar with the United Kingdom's postcode system, it identifies address areas based on population density. In the country-side, a postcode can cover an enormous expanse of land. For example, IV (Inverness) and SY (Shrewsbury) incorporate a lot of Scottish or Welsh mountains, while PA (Paisley) extends to several offshore islands.

My favourite postcode, BIQQ 1ZZ, refers to the entire British Antarctic Territory. Since this encompasses 650,000 square miles (1.7 million square kilometres), I'm glad we weren't trying to locate our stopover there!

Obviously, grid references and apps such as What3Words narrow things down considerably, but as we set our course for Cutthroat Bridge in the Peak District National Park, we hadn't considered such factors. Plus, like much of the British Antarctic Territory, to Mark and me, apps were a completely unexplored dominion.

We invested our faith in the satnav, which dutifully led us directly to the centre of the postcode. This was a point in the middle of nowhere, at least three miles from our destination. We arrived there via a track, which claimed to be, 'Unsuitable for HGVs' – something my husband tends to view more as a challenge than a warning.

It was an interesting drive.

The area is not called the Peak District for nothing. At Ughill, the country lane was just wide, straight, and flat enough for us to pull over and reconsider our questionable strategy. Desperate times call for desperate measures, and I felt so traumatised by the degree of 'interest' the drive involved that, for the first time ever, I used an app on my phone.

Google Maps located Cutthroat Bridge car park. It was on the main road, the A57, half a mile beyond where the satnav lured us off. After taking us on such an impressive and meandering journey to the centre of the postcode, the satnav deposited us on the A57 once again, two miles further back from where we started.

Although Cutthroat Bridge was so hard won, we decided not to stay. The car park presented an angle of slope perfect for making sure our kitchen drawers wouldn't stay closed.

Our mate Miles had conceived and built our kitchen with no

thought of how to prevent the drawers from flying open in transit. The day we embarked on our maiden voyage, he rushed into his workshop, swiftly crafted a stick with a spring screwed on top, and proudly issued the instruction, "Jam that through t'handles, wedge it under t'worktop, an' it will keep t'drawers shut."

Regarding a more sustainable long-term solution, he dismissed us with a cheery, "You'll need to get some child locks or something."

As with numerous other elements of our build, Miles' breezy response made it subtly clear. The puzzle of ensuring the drawers he designed remained closed was entirely ours to solve.

Even though we were in the Hope Valley, we felt disheartened. Not only because the drawers had nowhere to affix latches – that was a problem for another day. The stick/spring contraption worked passably, so the drawers functioned well so long as we didn't require access to the contents while parked on sloping terrain. At Cutthroat Bridge, that only ruled out cooking, drinking, and eating.

Rather, it was that overnight parking places are like toilets. When we had no need for one, we'd passed a plethora of lay-bys and rest areas, but now, in a moment of necessity, the one we'd found was out of order. We probably wouldn't find another until we'd wet and soiled ourselves. Speaking metaphorically, of course.

Yet, having finally lost my app virginity to Google Maps, I was on a roll. I had read about some useful apps on motorhome forums, so I downloaded Park4Night and discovered the Ladybower Inn, a pub just down the road. It charged £20 per night to stay overnight in its car park, but waived the charge if you had dinner.

Using feminine logic: a system of reasoning whose rationale states that a half-price dress bought for £50 represents a saving of £50, rather than a £50 expenditure, I figured The Ladybower was offering a £20 discount on a meal that didn't require me to cook or wash up. It was a no-brainer!

In addition, the pub was a gorgeous dun-coloured stone building, tucked into the hillside and festooned with purple wisteria. Even better, a sign outside claimed, 'Muddy Boots and Paws Welcome'. The car park was level, our drawers stayed shut, and a fur-friendly footpath led straight from the pub up onto the moors.

The Bull's Head in West Clandon, Surrey, serves my gold standard for steak pie. While The Ladybower couldn't topple its two-decade reign at Top of the Steak Pie Pops, it presented a worthy challenge.

Not only was the pie delicious, the beer was excellent, and the lovely staff proved very forthcoming with fuss and treats for The Fab Four, our travelling Cavapoodles. The following morning, we filled our lungs with the sharp green scent of bracken-after-the-rain as we took the pups up the steep rocky footpath behind the pub. I looked down upon the stupendous view of the Derwent Valley and Ladybower Reservoir with fresh eyes. A week into our new lorry life, my brain had begun to function somewhat differently.

"Mark, can you see that small track on the left of the reservoir? If we reversed down that, we could park there. Right on the lakeside..."

My wild-camping antenna was now fully activated!

But we had work to do in Halifax. Our window handles didn't clear the frames we'd built to accommodate our as-yet non-existent blinds, and wouldn't close properly, so we'd made an appointment with the supplier, Kellett Windows, to get them fixed.

En route, we needed to resupply. Doing your weekly shop in a truck requires a supermarket with a large car park: we set course for Sainsbury's in Grantham.

Since the symbol for Volvo represents iron, and Grantham is the birthplace of former British Prime Minister, Margaret Thatcher, I suggested,

"We could re-name The Beast 'The Iron Lady' after Maggie – the other Iron Lady of Grantham."

Unfortunately, as we headed towards our destination, our huge vintage Iron Lady caused a few concerns.

"What's that noise?" I asked Mark.

Seven days, two gas leaks, and one water leak into our travels, a lesson we'd already learned was: 'Never ignore strange noises or smells.'

Now, an ominous arrhythmic drumming sound had us on edge.

To guard against tree branches ripping off our solar panels, we'd fitted deflector bars to the roof of our cab. Finally, we identified them as the source. We'd tipped them with rubber, but every time we took a corner, they banged against the habitation box, and had already scraped off some paint.

In Halifax, we pulled up at a DIY megastore, where Mark hoped to grab a few parts to fix some minor issues – including a broken screen wash bottle. We suspected that Miles had kicked it accidentally while fitting the valves on the water tank – although he didn't mention it. The 30-year-old plastic was brittle, so the crack came as no surprise – and would probably have given way eventually. But it was classic Miles – like when he dropped his drill, shattered one of our discontinued nesting dog bowls, then cheerfully declared, "You'll need to get another one of those."

In a compact home, four identical bowls aren't a luxury – they are a necessity! Mismatched spares won't stack and store neatly, so we didn't need one replacement; we had to buy four.

Minor calamities, always ours to sort – and the latest, a dealbreaker for our mandatory MOT test at the end of the summer, wasn't exactly something we could fix easily via a high-street ironmonger.

While I waited with the pooches, The Beast gathered a small crowd from around Jane and Graham's snack van.

The chip butty (chip sandwich) is possibly the greatest north-of-England delicacy. The recipe is simple: a row of proper thick-cut chips – none of your spindly, extruded French fries – seasoned with salt and brown malt vinegar, squished between two heavily buttered pieces of white sliced bread. Or a white roll, if you're posh.

Jane and Graham supplied two of their 'famous chip butties' – with the genius incorporation of pulled beef and gravy. Without a doubt, it was the most exceptional chip butty I've ever had!

After one chap in our crowd of admirers told us all about his hippy days, when he travelled in an old bus, Jane said,

"I lived in a Transit van with my boyfriend for two years. Back in the day, I toured on a yacht. I visited Spain, Italy, and Romania. Romania was properly dodgy in those days!"

"We love Romania!" we replied. "We visited a few years ago and now it's one of our favourite countries."

Eventually, after lunch, we found Kellet Windows, but not before we'd rumbled and twisted through a maze of narrow cobbled streets designed to accommodate nineteenth-century horses and carts as opposed to twentieth-century 6-wheel military trucks.

I found it such a pleasure to meet the owner, Victoria, at last. During the build, we'd spoken so many times on the phone. A cheerful chat with Vic always gave us a lift that lasted all day – something we'd needed desperately in those dark times of unending stress and impending homelessness.

Michael, Kellet's chief engineer, soon fixed the windows simply by slicing the ends off the handles to shorten them. Afterwards, in the spirit of Kellet's 'service beyond the call of duty', he clambered up on The Beast's roof with an angle grinder and removed a chunk from the deflector bars to stop the banging. In the meantime, Vic and I had a chat. She made me a cup of tea and asked where we might stay that night.

"We've no idea!" I replied.

"Hebden Bridge is lovely," she said.

So we went there.

Chapter 5

That Was So Hebden Bridge

'Lovely' is certainly not how Sir Bernard Ingham, former Prime Minister Margaret Thatcher's press secretary, described his hometown.

In his column in *The Hebden Bridge Times*, he declared it tantamount to Sodom and Gomorrah.

Starkly northern, its smoke-blackened stone buildings, varnished with rain, still cling to precipitous valley sides. However, in recent history, the town gave itself a somewhat unconventional makeover.

During the 1800s, Hebden Bridge was such a thriving centre for clothing manufacture, it earned the nickname 'Trouser Town'. Sheep grazing the barren moorland above supplied wool, while fast-flowing streams rushing down from the Pennine hills provided the perfect power-source for cloth-making mills. It was famous for fustian, a type of heavy corduroy used to make workwear fit for real men.

Sadly, by the 1960s, the industry had declined, and 'Fustianopolis' deteriorated into a slum. As property prices plummeted, squatters, artists, and hippies moved in. Then, in a clash of tie-dye and tweed, these 'offcumdens', as locals call outsiders, formed a community group. They cleaned up and preserved the old buildings, and enabled HB – Hebden Bridge – to rise like a phoenix of alternative culture from the ashes of its industrial heritage.

These days, you need a lottery win to buy a property, while Fustian and Phoenix are more likely to be a gender-neutral couple running a café in the square serving vegan treats for cats. The expression, 'Getting the bus to Hebden Bridge' means coming out as a lesbian, because this little place in the heart of the Calder Valley, with around 4,500 residents, is the self-proclaimed lesbian capital of Great Britain.

Yet one commentator's description of HB as 'a drug town with a tourist problem' could explain some of Sir Bernard Ingham's gripes. *Happy Valley*, a TV drama set and filmed in the area, took its title from the nickname used by police because of widespread substance abuse.

However, there are many more positives.

In 2011, British Airways' *High Life* magazine named Hebden Bridge the fourth quirkiest town in the world!

Hebden Bridge boasts even more cafés per head of population than it does beardy blokes with straggly ponytails or man buns. It prides itself on its range of independent shops. So, if you're running low on anything handmade, eco-friendly, renewable, sustainable, or farm fresh, HB is your baby. Likewise, if you want to workshop your inner wizard, discover your wild woman within, or line dance with your ancestors before you stock up on fair-trade fridge magnets and ethical ear muffs crafted from locally foraged lichen, squirrel poo, and repurposed barbed wire, this is the place to come.

I once heard about a woman in Barrow-in-Furness who offered rebirthing. Armed only with some drain pipes and a tin of castor oil, she'd pop you in at one end, and leave you to work your way through. Then, she'd slap you on the bum, give you a spoon of castor oil, and you were reborn.

In Hebden Bridge, she'd fit right in.

As we drove our huge lorry camper past the cafés, looking for a stopover, Mark spied a couple of rainbow-haired hippies at a bus stop.

"They look like they might know somewhere we could park tonight," he said, as he pulled over and addressed them from on high in the cab.

"There's a spot up the road that opens out onto a woodland," they said, before sending us on our way in a wave of patchouli-scented directions.

Perfect!

Except here was a lesson.

The public at large radically underestimates the size of our vehicle.

Their instructions led us up a narrow, twisting street with cars parked on either side. Half a mile in, we stopped to stare at an unfortunate inconvenience. Between us and our arboreal Nirvana stood a belligerently low railway bridge.

The Beast is 12′ 6″ (3.85 m) high.

"You'll never get under that!" I stated the obvious, but we were already down the rabbit hole. The Beast is also 33 ft (10 m) long, so at this point, neither could we turn around.

Our van, Big Blue and Caravan Kismet, which in tandem comprised our previous home-on-wheels, were the length of an articulated lorry. Wordlessly, as had happened so often in our travels, I swung down from the passenger seat, pulled on a Hi-Vis waistcoat, and guided Mark backwards. Then I strode manfully into the middle of the main road to halt the traffic while he reversed out.

Unsure what to do once we'd extricated ourselves, we headed towards Hebden Bridge and its cafés once again. The populace spilled out onto the pavements in the late afternoon sunshine. We would have loved to join them, but there was nowhere to stop.

Every time we rounded a bend, our newly shortened deflector bars still played a low frequency timpanic solo on the roof behind the cab. En route to the woods, I had spotted a garage on the near side of the road.

"Look. Red lorry, yellow lorry!" I'd joked, referencing two magnificent bull-nosed trucks they had on display.

As we passed it on the way back, I had to lunge for the inner door pull to steady myself as Mark slewed across the oncoming carriageway to reach the forecourt.

Mark was half way out of the cab as he announced, "I'm going to see if they've got an angle grinder we can borrow."

A crowd of mechanics in navy blue overalls crawled like oil-spattered zombies out of the inspection pit and gathered to admire The Beast. Although it was near closing time on a Friday, they were amenable to Mark's curious request. In these early days, another truck truth we were discovering was how much our magnificent Beast opens doors.

On the grounds of 'Elf and Safety', they declined to clamber nearly two storeys up onto The Beast's roof, wielding a power tool. However, they granted Mark the freedom to risk his own life and limbs, and deploy their angle grinder at his altitude of choice.

The blade wasn't big enough to slice fully through the stainless-steel bars, so Mark had to finish the cuts with a hacksaw. I remained on *terra firma,* chatting about The Beast with one mechanic, who took me over to see the bull nosed trucks.

"The red one does stunts," he said. "It's a wheelie truck."

"No way!" I replied, and decided on the spot not to tell Mark, lest he viewed it as a challenge similar to road signs which declare, 'Unsuitable for Heavy Goods Vehicles'.

As we drove back into town, we realised that, despite its ardour for alternative lifestyles, Hebden Bridge couldn't accommodate those choosing to do so on wheels.

I felt all in. It was 6 p.m. and we'd been on the road since 9 a.m. Shattered. Demoralised. Driving around aimlessly in a huge truck, wondering where on earth we could spend the night.

Despite being a complete virgin only the day before, I was getting rather nimble with my apps. With our ever-shortening roof deflectors, we set off in search of a cricket club in nearby Mytholmroyd, which promised a Park4Night right on the banks of the Rochdale Canal. It was a short walk from Hebden Bridge, and close to a very famous address.

West Yorkshire boasts a notable literary legacy. Just a few miles over the moors lay Howarth, whose vicarage was home to the Brontë sisters, Charlotte, Emily, and Anne. A vet called James Alfred Wight wrote about his life in the area. Known more famously as James Herriot, several TV series were based on his bestselling books, including *All Creatures Great and Small*. And who could forget Takayoshi Andoh's inimitable *Memoirs of a Japanese Chicken Sexer in 1935 Hebden Bridge*?

And yes. That is a real book.

A hawk's stoop from The Beast's doorstep lay 1, Aspinall Street, Mytholmroyd, where poet laureate Ted Hughes was born. He married the American writer, Sylvia Plath, in 1956, although when you read their poems, a happy couple living in Happy Valley seems a long shot. They separated just six years later, in 1962, when Hughes started an affair. Then in 1963, aged only 30, Plath committed suicide. Her grave is in nearby Heptonstall, where feminists frequently chisel off the

'Hughes' part of her surname from her gravestone.[1]

From bed, our view was the Rochdale Canal, where Hughes fished as a child. Together with the surrounding Pennine moors and its wildlife, the canal featured in much of Hughes' poetry.

The next day, in what I can only describe as grey mizzle, we hiked along the sodden canal into Hebden Bridge. In a fug of earthy summer smells released by the rain, The Fab Four splashed joyfully through puddles on the black cinder towpath, which ran parallel to the River Calder and the main Burnley Road. Derelict narrowboats lined the canal. A damp patina of moss and mould decorated their faded turquoise and purple paintwork. With Buddhas on their roofs and dreamcatchers in their windows, they were the New Age community's floating antidote to the area's unaffordable property prices. The throbbing generator of one moored next to our park-up had lulled us to sleep.

The Rochdale canal is an incredible feat of engineering. In 1804, it became the first of three trans-Pennine waterways to open, winning the race to cross the hills called 'the backbone of England.' It connects the city of Manchester with Sowerby Bridge in Calderdale. By going straight over the top, it bypassed the issues with tunnels which bedevilled its rivals, the Leeds-Liverpool and Huddersfield Narrow Canals. Although it is only 32 miles (51.5 km) long, the steep climb required 91 locks.

Despite this, the Huddersfield Narrow beat the Rochdale to the title of highest canal in Britain by 45 ft (13.7 m), and the Bingley 'Five Rise' on the Leeds-Liverpool claims the steepest flight of locks.

---

1. Silvia Plath's headstone has been vandalised so frequently that the lettering was replaced in bronze, which is easier to repair.

The Huddersfield Narrow Canal also holds the record as the highest, longest, and deepest canal tunnel in the UK. It took sixteen years to complete, but at an altitude of 645 ft (187 m) and a maximum depth of 638 ft (194 m), the Standedge Tunnel gouged its way beneath the Pennine summits for 3.5 miles (5.6 km).

At Hawksclough, cars swished past on wet tarmac as we paused under dripping trees to admire a rusting cast iron sculpture. A hawk hunched on a tall tree stump, gripping a small bird in its talons. It references the Ted Hughes poem, *Hawk Roosting:* an uplifting meditation on the joys of ripping off heads. Apparently, Hughes was inspired while playing in Red Acre Wood with his childhood friend, Donald Crossley. There, they observed a hawk going about its grisly business, oblivious to the momentous contribution it would one day make to English Literature.

A squat factory chimney and the blank four-storey edifices of industrial buildings lined our moist approach into Hebden Bridge. Built from dressed blocks of coarse-grained local sandstone called millstone grit, regiments of tall windows punctuated the taupe-coloured facades. Once dark satanic mills, they are now home to fancy restaurants, purveyors of craft beer, or expensive canal-side apartments for the well-to-do of Leeds and Manchester.

Given its trio of watercourses (two natural, one man-made), Hebden Bridge could justifiably rebrand itself as 'Hebden Bridges'. But when we left the canal and entered the town, we walked over THE Hebden Bridge. Two of its three elegant arches span Hebden Water, a tributary of the River Calder. In very HB style, the third soars majestically over dry land, but this is because it spanned the Goit, a watercourse for the mill, which was filled in as the conurbation expanded.

The area's gritstone is prized for its durability, and this particular rocky road has survived the Yorkshire climate since 1510. We crossed the cobbled walkway, iron grey and slick with rain, and plonked ourselves down on outside chairs to partake of coffee and a cake in the dry, as rain pattered gently on the café's awning.

As Mark went inside to order, I chatted with a lady at the next table.

"Hebden Bridge is famous for dock pudding," she told me. "Every April, they hold the World Dock Pudding Championships at the leisure centre in Mytholmroyd."

"I've heard of Yorkshire Pudding, but not dock pudding," I replied. "What is it?"

"It's a local delicacy made from a special kind of dock leaf, mixed with stinging nettles, oatmeal, and onions."

"Stinging nettles?!" That sounded so Hebden Bridge.

"Yes – it's usually one-third dock to two-thirds nettles, but everyone has their own 'mystery ingredients'. It's fried in bacon fat and served as part of a traditional Yorkshire breakfast, with bacon, sausages, and egg."

When I looked it up later, I found that in 'the olden days' dock pudding was an important source of vitamin C. By spring, the population was on the brink of scurvy after a winter eating only preserved vegetables. 'Sweet' or 'Passion' docks and tender nettle tops were the first greens to come through. Residents mixed them with whatever else was available, such as sorrel, spinach, chives, or raspberry leaves.

Hebden Bridge's dock pudding made it on to German radio during WWII.

Propagandist William Joyce, better known as Lord Haw Haw, reported that food rationing was so bad that Yorkshire was eating grass!

Actor Robbie Coltrane, who played Hagrid in the *Harry Potter* films, came second in the 2007 Dock Pudding Championship. In 2013, the Yorkshire weather caused the event to be cancelled. It was too wet for the Bistort docks to grow, so they held a car boot sale instead. But in 2004, there was outrage when Jetta, a Danish chef who worked in one of HB's many cafés, won first prize with a vegetarian version.

It caused an uproar!

"Bacon is an essential ingredient!" the townspeople raged. "Traditional dock pudding is intrinsically NOT vegetarian."

With impeccable Hebden Bridge logic, Jetta argued that forty per cent of residents were vegetarian. She maintained that if you wanted to keep old traditions alive, you had to move with the times.

Jetta kept her prize, although I found an unverified account that in 2017, the judges disqualified a vegan dock pudding...

Back at the cricket pitch, the groundsman asked us politely to move, because the club had a match the following day.

We secured our belongings, then roared up the narrow lanes and along the balcony roads that led out of town. From Hebden Bridge, the only way is up.

As we ascended, we passed the distinctive gritstone terraces of weavers' cottages that grace the lush green hillsides.

Ever the innovator, even before Hebden Bridge pioneered the notion of chakra alignment via the medium of shamanic chanting accompanied by a white witch strumming a ukulele, it embraced the concept of 'flying freehold'. This grants Happy Valley residents the legal right to live on the ceiling!

With so little flat building land available in the steep-sided valley with its marshy floor, Hebden Bridge came up with a typically unorthodox solution. The distinctive 'Top and Bottom Houses' are four- or five-storey buildings, split horizontally. Facing in opposite directions, the two residences have street entrances at different levels. The Bottom House, which opens onto the lower street, owns the shared floor/ceiling outright, but a flying freehold legally grants the Top House the right to live on it!

And so, with our deflector bars duly shortened with a borrowed angle grinder, filled with appreciation for Hebden Bridge's trailblazing tendencies, and in awe of the controversy that a vegan version of a vegetable delicacy made from stinging nettles could foment, we noticed the town's farewell sign.

Thanking careful drivers or wishing you a pleasant onward trip would never cut it in the planet's fourth funkiest place.

In lettering to match the way markers on its 500-year-old bridge, the boundary sign neatly declared,

'That Was So Hebden Bridge'.

Chapter 6

Bridestones

With no further overnight parking opportunities within Hebden Bridge itself, we set off in search of a couple of lay-bys I'd found on the shores of a nearby reservoir. We ground up hills and wound through the crazed patchwork of the Pennines, criss-crossed with grey, lichen-covered dry-stone walls. Bemused-looking sheep and cattle examined us as we held our breath and squeezed past oncoming cars, and the occasional truck, amid a maze of narrow and precipitous country lanes.

Inevitably, the road we needed to take was closed for resurfacing. It always happens to us. I looked at the map and sighed.

"Mark, it's another Lake Bohinj."

In a remote part of Slovenia, similarly lacking a density of thoroughfares, a road closure stopped us less than a mile (1.6 km) from our destination and forced us to take a million-mile diversion around three sides of a square to approach from the other side.

On top of the fells, unencumbered by the steep valley sides, at least I had internet. A Christmas tree symbol on Park4Night intimated there was a lay-by nearby, so we headed for that. I prayed it would be suitable.

The lay-by was more than suitable. It was absolutely beautiful.

On the very summit of the moors, it was right next to The Bride-stones, a striking outcrop of Jurassic sandstone pillars, shaped by wind and rain into fantastical shapes. The space was level-ish, but improved by Mark getting one side of The Beast up on a few bricks that were lying around.

As we settled ourselves in, I noticed a lone figure in a blue anorak gazing intently at us from the stile that crossed the dry-stone wall over the road. He stared for some time before he wandered over to explain,

"I'm Patrick. I toured Africa in a ZIL, a Soviet version of your truck!"

To give our pooches a leg stretch, we walked up to the Bridestone rocks with Patrick and Blue, his border collie. On the way, Patrick told us a bit about the history and folklore that surrounded the stones.

"The stones formed 150-million years ago, when dinosaurs still roamed the earth!"

We marvelled at the Great Bridestone, which looks like an upturned oval bottle, balancing precariously on its narrow neck. The Groom Stone lies next to his 15 ft (4.6 m) high bride.

"Local people toppled him over some time in the 17th century, probably because the church thought pagan rituals took place here. Although people were reputedly married at the Bridestones, historians think the name came from the local Brigantes tribe, who named the stones after their goddess, Briganta. She was also known as Brighid, Brigha, or Bridia. The other stones have names, too."

Patrick pointed out the Anvil, the Sphinx, and, um, the Obscene Cleft.

Of course, Ted Hughes wrote about the stones. His poem *Bride-stones* features in the collection, *Remains of Elmet*. Founded by King Mascuid the Lame when the Romans withdrew, Elmet was reputedly the last Celtic kingdom to fall to the Angles. Although Northumbria conquered Elmet around 616, a 2015 study published in the journal *Nature* noted that the population of that part of West Yorkshire remained genetically distinct from the rest of Yorkshire – and indeed, England – and could be descendants of the Elmetsæte.

Patrick was quite the nomad himself. He told us,

"I do HelpX; it's a workaway like WWOOF-ing (World Wide Opportunities on Organic Farms), but with bells on!"

He had spent months at a time out of the UK, working on various projects. A true traveller, he immediately offered the use of his bath (the one home comfort I miss because of our nomadic lifestyle!) and to drive us into town if we needed supplies. As the conversation progressed, he posed a challenging question.

"What does home mean to you?"

It was genuinely difficult to answer.

Mark couldn't really say.

For me, who moved house over twenty-five times before I became a perpetual vagabond, home is The Beast – or wherever the pups and Mark are. I explained,

"I don't feel a strong affiliation with any place. My original hometown is Blackburn, but I no longer belong there. I left for university when I was seventeen and have lived predominantly in the south since then. Other than Dad and a few friends, I have little connection with the town."

Then, I returned the favour and asked Patrick what home meant to him.

"Home for me is here at Bridestones, although I have a motorhome and a holiday place in Ireland."

He said his favourite answer to his question came from a guy who placed his hands across his chest, close to his heart, and said, "Home is in here."

By the time we'd played Lorry Life Bingo with our neighbour, Dave, another full-time motor homer, and two ladies with cocker spaniels who came to look inside The Beast, it was nearly 9 p.m.

I cooked a stir-fry as we watched the sunset. The sky softened over the barren moors, although twinkling lights from scattered hill farms added a cosiness to the stark landscape. The chattering of crickets and the plaintive cries of curlew provided the soundscape as a barn owl flitted silently across the field next to us.

It was bliss.

Curiously, as I observed the scene, Patrick's question, 'What does home mean to you?' answered itself. I suddenly experienced a strong sense of belonging to this wild moorland landscape, which was so reminiscent of the Lancashire countryside where I spent my childhood.

'Aleatory' had popped up as Word of the Day in my inbox. It means:

1. In law; depending on chance, luck, or an uncertain outcome, e.g. an aleatory contract.

2. Relating to accidental causes, luck, or chance, e.g. an aleatory element.

3. In music; employing an element of chance in tones, rhythm, or dynamics.

I was already getting used to our increasingly aleatory existence.

Initially, I had found driving around aimlessly in a large vehicle with nowhere to go terrifying.

Now, as I looked over a view that you couldn't buy for a million pounds, I appreciated the possibilities our lorry life opened up.

I absolutely loved the freedom.

And soon, we would meet some more of Elmet's colourful locals...

Chapter 7

How To Make A Four Month Trip Last Fourteen Years!

I have written this chapter in the vernacular. I hope it makes sense. If you struggle with the Yorkshire dialect, just for fun, there is a short Yorkshire/English glossary at the end!

"Mark. We didn't run anyone over when we parked, did we?"

As Mark and I descended the steps at 9 a.m. on Sunday morning, two pairs of legs, clad in bright orange high-visibility overalls, were sticking out from beneath our truck.

As we clattered down the steps, the legs spoke.

"Eyup! Ah didn't realise there were anyone in!"

A slim, grey-haired chap slid out from beneath the truck, followed shortly by his stockier, black-haired mate. Both sporting full Hi-Vis onesies.

"We were lookin' at yer axles! Ah heard voices and thought Ah better introduce meself!" the older gentleman addressed me. "Tek this down, lass. You know how to do Google and that, don't ya? Look me up; 'Ian Coates Honda'. Ah can do work on this truck. This is me apprentice, Willie. 'E's in 'is fifties now though. Ah'm seventy-five!"

That was our introduction to Yorkshire's equivalent of Fred Dibnah, Lancashire's highly colourful and much-loved old-school steeplejack-cum-steam-traction-engine guru who had his own television series, simply called *Fred*.

We invited Ian and Willie in for a brew (a cup of tea), for which they reciprocated with truck wisdom and entertainment. Ian shared his life story,

"Ah'll tell ya this. A bloke asked me to go to get 'is motorbike from Johannesburg. Ah said, 'wheer's Johannesburg? Is it in Wales?' 'E said, 'No, it's in Africa!' So, Ah said, 'Wheer's it near?' 'E said, 'Cape Town.'

"Well, Ah said to me missus, 'Ah'll be gone four month,' so Ah set off and got tuh Africa. Ah went along a bit, then a country wouldn't let me in. Ah stopped at a shop wi' a phone and rang t'bloke wi' t'motorbike. 'What country you in?' he asked. Ah asked lass in t'shop. 'Kenya,' she said. 'What town,' 'e asked. 'Nairobi' It were Sudan wouldn't let me in.

"Well, Ah thought, there's me motorbike in t'cowshed, so Ah phoned our lad and said, 'Pack that up and send it tuh Nairobi.' Then Ah phoned our lass an' said, 'Ah'm gonna be gone longer than four month!'

"Ah went round Africa for four year on me bike! Ah went to Johannesburg, then Malawi an' Namibia. Ah nipped into Sudan – under t'radar, like. Then Ah asked, 'Wheer's Egypt?' Ah didn't 'ave a map. Yuh don't need a map.

"Then, Ah asked, 'Wheer's Argentina?' So, Ah had me bike shipped out there! There were snow on t'ground. Silly buggers there 'ave winter in July! Ah asked, 'Wheer's Alaska? Ah'm gonna go there!' So, Ah rode me bike all t'way up America. Ah were gone fourteen year!"

"You were gone for fourteen years!" Mark and I exclaimed. "What on earth did your wife think?"

"Judith? Eeeh, when Ah got back, she 'ad a face like a bulldog suckin' piss off a thistle!"

Ian shared some tips on safety while travelling. Pointing at me, he said,

"When someone comes knockin' by surprise, you need to say, 'Oh. Ah thought it were Frank. I'm expecting Frank and 'is son.' Then they'll think you've got someone comin' and you'll be safe."

After tea, we all went back outside. Willie had a look under the hood and showed Mark how to use the tyre inflator that runs off the brake compressors. He also told us we need to grease our nipples weekly. Mark and I caught each other's gaze. We didn't know we had nipples to grease, but we do love a double entendre.

The next surreal moment of the day was when Ian and Willie took Mark off to see their workshop. I found myself sitting in the truck with the dogs all alone, with no phone, because that was in Mark's pocket. I locked the door and spent the next ninety minutes wondering whether they had actually kidnapped my husband. If they had, I was well and truly stuck. Due to coronavirus lockdowns, I'd been unable to apply for a licence, which precluded having any truck driving lessons.

You get a feeling about people, and I reckoned Ian and Willie were good eggs, although I noted the registration number of Ian's Land Rover. Just in case.

In due course, Mark returned with Ian and his wife Judith, a grease gun ("a solid one you can ram right in"), and a couple of tubes of grease.

Ian stared at me with eyes like lasers. "Who are you expectin'?" he asked.

"Frank!" I replied.

"And?" Ian didn't drop his gaze.

"Frank and 'is son!"

"Good lass!" Ian beamed.

They both came in for a cuppa. Judith was a sweetheart. A tiny slender lady with a serene face, framed by wispy grey hair, swept back into a ponytail. Her gentle demeanour belied a core of quiet Yorkshire grit. I asked her,

"How did you get on with him gone for fourteen years?!"

"Oh. It were alright!" She sighed. "Ah 'ad me kids and grandkids. An' Ah used to fly out and meet 'im every now and again."

I got the impression she had quite enjoyed the peace.

Clearly, the meeting at Ian's place had gone swimmingly. "You should see his yard," Mark told me. "It's amazing!"

Then Mark laughed as he prompted Ian,

"Tell Jackie why they threw you out of Kazakhstan."

With a massive grin and twinkling eyes, Ian told the tale.

"Well, Ah got to't border and Ah were all set. They stamped me passport and everythin', then they asked what Ah was wantin' to do there, so Ah told 'em. 'Ah've come to see wheer Borat lived.'

"And they chucked me out!

"Ah spoke to me mate and told 'im, 'They chucked me out o'Kazakhstan!'

"'E said, 'Yer didn't mention Borat did yer?'

"So Ah said, 'Ah did!' and 'e said, 'Yer daft 'apeth!'"

In case you're not familiar, *Borat* is a controversial mockumentary comedy film whose lead character, Borat Sagdiyev, is an anti-Semitic Kazakh journalist, played by actor Sacha Baron Cohen. Personally, I love Baron Cohen's trademark of shockingly exaggerated characters who poke fun at racism and prejudice. However, it does not make him popular in all circles. Particularly those who take British satire and self-deprecating humour at face value.

Kazakhstan and Russia banned the film *Borat*. According to the news agency Pravda, the film left the Kazakhs feeling furious and humiliated, and Baron Cohen received death threats.

Ian's travels had taken him to almost every country in the world. He told us all kinds of stories. At one point, he told us he was teaching English in a girls' school.

"Ah taught 'em to sing '*On Ilkley Moor Bah t'At*'. That took about two week. After that, Ah taught 'em '*The Lassie from Lancashire*' – then Ah thought, 'Oh no! Ah've taught 'em to sing it in a Yorkshire accent! But Ah don't reckon anyone would know.'"

There is a fierce rivalry between the northern English counties of Lancashire and Yorkshire. It goes back all the way to the Wars of the Roses between 1455 and 1487, when the houses of York and Lancaster battled it out for the British throne. It ended when Henry Tudor slaughtered the last king standing, Richard III, at the Battle of Bosworth Field.

The Lancashire/Yorkshire rivalry applies in all instances, unless Lankies and Yorkies come together 'Down South', in which case, we all identify as 'Northerners' and present a united front in opposition to the Southern Shandy-drinking Softies!

In addition to a grease gun, Mark came back with a list of maintenance tasks. In my innocence, I had believed that the truck was similar to a car, and only required an annual service.

"Tek this down, lass," Ian instructed. "You need to mek a list of spares and maintenance things and tick it off when it's done to keep track. If you don't keep yer nipples greased, yer prop shaft can seize. If owt else goes wrong, you can still drive. But if yer prop shaft goes, yer well and truly stuck..."

Mark revelled in his newfound knowledge regarding which of the six were the drive wheels. Like the rest of her, The Beast's tyres looked brand new. Although 30-years old, they had done fewer than 3,100 miles (5,000 km). Ian explained the new regulations for coaches and lorries, which would require the tyres on the steering wheels to be fewer than ten years old. That was thrilling news; we had thought the regs applied to all tyres, so it meant we only needed to change the two front tyres, rather than the full half dozen. As yet, we had no inkling of the tyre-related Pandora's Box that lay in wait. Ian hinted at it as he pressed home the benefit of us carrying both spare wheels. "You have split-rim wheels. They call them 'widow makers'. They have to be inflated in a cage. If you get a puncture, no-one will want to change one of those at t'roadside."

So, besides greasing our nipples weekly – or possibly monthly with our mileage – we needed to stock up on Type 30 brake diaphragms, bleed the brake air tanks daily – or weekly with our mileage – to get rid of water condensed in the tanks, and change our front tyres in the next few months, before the new legislation came in.

Mark and I gave ourselves a virtual high five.

We had a maintenance schedule and knew our drive wheels from our steering wheels. We were really getting the hang of this truckin' mullarkey.

Or so we thought.

***

Yorkshire/English Translation

- **Tenses** – In Yorkshire dialect, verb tenses and participles are mixed around, e.g. **Ah were doin' summat** instead of 'I was doing something', or **I was stood** instead of I was standing.

- **Dropped Letters**

  - Letters are often dropped from the beginning and end of words, such as **'E** (He) and **Goin'** (Going).

  - Aitches are always dropped.

  - Plurals – the S is frequently dropped, so 'four months' becomes 'four month'.

- **Pronunciation** – think professional Yorkshireman, actor Sean Bean!

Glossary

- **Ah** – I

- **Apeth** – Literally a Halfpenneth or Halfpennyworth, but used as an affectionate term for a silly person, as in 'you daft apeth'.

- **Aht** – Out or outside

- **Bloke** – Man

- **Brew** – Cup of Tea

- **Eyup!** – 'Hello', or an exclamation along the lines of Flipping Heck!

- **Lass** – Girl *(see also **Ahr lass** below)*

- **Me** – My

- **Mek** – Make

- **Meself** – Myself

- **Missus** – Wife

- **On Ilkley Moor Baht 'At** – On Ilkley Moor without a hat; Yorkshire's unofficial anthem

- **Ahr lad** – 'Our lad' – means my son

- **Ahr lass** – 'Our girl' – my wife

- **Owt** – Anything (Nowt is nothing)

- **T'** – The. Sometimes the definite article is also dropped completely, as in – 'I asked lass in t'shop'

- **Tek** – Take

- **Tuh** – To

- **Wheer** – Where

- **Ya** – You

- **Yer** – You or Your

Chapter 8

Bridestones to Ingleton

I t was a challenging day, not only because of the narrow roads and hairpin bends that led from Ted Hughes and Brontë country into Herriot country, directly away from *Last of the Summer Wine* country.[1]

We stopped for lunch in a verdant lay-by and got chatting to a chap who'd had the same idea, although the conversation took a bit of a wrong turn when he brought up COVID vaccinations.

The subject arose with talk of vaccine passports and going abroad. A pipe dream at the time, with all international travel banned because of the pandemic.

---

1. *Last of the Summer Wine* is a long-running British sitcom about three eccentric old Yorkshiremen whose madcap adventures gently poke fun at ageing, friendship, and rural life. Episodes usually conclude with them hurtling down a hillside in a bathtub or some such!

The man expressed some concern about the coronavirus vaccine, and Mark said, "You need to ask Jackie about that. She's a biochemist."

I proffered some reassurance about how vaccination works and the means by which scientists developed the COVID-19 jab so quickly, but he immediately started to mansplain, putting forward some startlingly innovative theories of his own.

"They've looked at it, Spanish professors an' all, and they said t'jab is less than one per cent virus parts. It's full of graphene! Elon Musk says graphene can coat your brain, then they can input electronic messages and mek you do what they want. And they can hear your thoughts!

"You should have a look at graphene on ShoeTube. (A broad Yorkshireman, he pronounced it Shyaw Tyawb). It's like YouTube, but it's where all t'people went who got banned from YouTube because they don't agree wi't' government."

He was very strident. I'm a girl, and things you've seen on ShoeTube obviously carry much more weight than a BSc (Hons) degree from a British university, so he was perfectly justified in talking over me and ignoring any point I made.

I tried to be polite and interjected with an occasional, "I can't agree with you there," and "I would be interested to see the peer-reviewed scientific papers that document the research these highly respected 'professors an' all' in Spain have carried out."

He continued with, "But what about this? 1,500 people who've had t'vaccine have died!"

I had to counter with, "Well, no vaccine is one hundred per cent effective, but in the UK alone, 150,000 unvaccinated people have died of COVID-19."

He was not having that. He yelled his reply back at me, showering me with spittle.

"NO, THEY HAVEN'T! THEY DIED OF A POSITIVE PCR TEST!"

By this stage, he was actually frothing at the mouth. His mild-mannered wife looked on with a serene smile from her picnic chair and continued grazing like a contented bovine from a Tupperware box filled with salad.

"Well. We'd best be getting on our way. How lovely to meet you," I said, while thinking, *If you are ever diagnosed with diabetes, for example, and refuse to take insulin, I'm sure you'd be happy to say you died from a blood sugar test, and had a lucky escape from Elon Musk turning you into a cyborg.*

The coronavirus pandemic was like a lightning rod to conspiracy theories. Fuelled by social media and a desperate need to rationalise and understand the tragedy as it unfolded, rumours spread as rapidly as the virus itself. One of the earliest and most persistent rumours claimed the virus was manmade and released by a shadowy elite as part of a global plot.

Elon Musk and his graphene were new to me. However, tech giants such as Microsoft and Bill Gates using the COVID-19 vaccine as a tool to implant microchips to enable them to control or track the population was old news. Conspiracists blamed the 5G phone network for weakening the immune system, or even spreading the virus, and had vandalised some phone masts. And in the meantime, others even blamed Big Pharma for creating the disease to profit from selling vaccines – while promoting their own expensive 'miracle pills' that would cure all known ills, including COVID-19.

Yet, arguing with a conspiracy theorist feels like being caught in a never-ending maze. Questioning the conspiracy immediately makes you complicit. You're either an ignorant, naïve sheep, who has been duped by the establishment, or worse, you're part of the coverup.

Then, the lack of credible evidence proves how clever the conspiracy is, because it's covered its tracks.

This circular logic makes it impossible to debate. Any contradiction serves only to strengthen the believer's conviction, because they are enlightened and 'in the know'. Challenging them when they see themselves as guardians of truth in a deceptive world makes you a brainwashed, uneducated moron.

But then, maybe I am.

There's so much misinformation out there, it's difficult to identify what is true.

In time, the extent to which governments and individuals profited from the pandemic would come to light, and when it did, that was as shocking as any conspiracy.

***

We arrived late at our destination, even though our journey was only about 60 miles (96 km). The Beast is slow and the roads were haphazard. My camera broke, so I launched myself beyond apps, even further into the modern age. I started snapping photos from my phone and uploading them directly to social media, completely bypassing my laptop.

For accuracy, Mongolian horse archers would time loosing their arrows into the fleeting moment when all four hooves of a galloping horse left the ground. The Beast was so bumpy with her growling engine and knobbly tyres that I had to synchronise my photographic efforts with the brief stillness after Mark's gear changes had hurled me around. Otherwise, my captures of the undulating yellow-green moorland, criss-crossed with dry-stone walls and dotted with grey, no-nonsense farmsteads, came out blurred.

We chose to park for the night in a large lay-by on the moors above the quaint little town of Ingleton.

It was sensational.

Just inside the Yorkshire Dales National Park, a path led directly from our door to the distinctively flat summit of Ingleborough, a limestone behemoth thought to have been the site of an Iron Age hillfort. With the evening drawing in, we took the pups part way up the mountain for an evening leg stretch. We met a lovely family on their descent from the summit, although they were having a few issues. The soles had come off Sue's boots, and her husband, Steve, had been forced to climb back up to retrieve his drone, which had gone out of range. Sue, a kindred spirit, also wanted to ride horses in Mongolia. They were both very interested in our lifestyle.

"You are living our dream!" they said.

Our life of freedom is a dream for many.

We told them, "We are proof that it is achievable, if you plan and set your mind to it."

***

At 2,372 ft (723 m), Ingleborough is the second highest of the famous Yorkshire Three Peaks: the object of a popular challenge – a 24-mile (38.6 km) round trip to ascend all three in 12 hours.

The Yorkshire Three Peaks is distinct from the National Three Peaks Challenge, which is a 24-hour dash to climb Snowdon, Scafell Pike, and Ben Nevis: the highest peaks in Wales, England, and Scotland.

Aged around seven, I conquered Ingleborough's compatriots,

Pen-y-ghent and Whernside, in the same day. I was with my dad, a teacher, charged with shepherding a school group around all three. Marshalling duties denied us Ingleborough, so it remains a long-standing piece of unfinished business for me.

"I wonder if I can still claim my Three Peaks badge after taking fifty years to complete the challenge?"

Mark gave me a look.

"It might be a record!" I protested.

The weather had improved markedly. We were expecting a heat-wave the following day and decided on an early start so that I could finally bag my third summit.

Back at the truck, a magnificent sunset lit up far-reaching views across Morecambe Bay. We could see Coniston in the Lake District, and the glistening towers of the nuclear power station at Heysham Head.

Our only neighbours were sheep, and thankfully, they didn't have opinions to share about COVID vaccines.

Chapter 9

Ingleton: Home of the Shewee

O n Ingleton's tourism websites, you'll read about 'the land of waterfalls and caves'. It's an outdoor Mecca, famous for hiking, biking, and spelunking, as friends 'over the pond' might refer to activities undertaken by a certain strange breed of subterranean thrill seekers. Those like my university caving club, who sported t-shirts with 'Happiness Is a Tight Wet Hole' emblazoned across their chests.

But I aim to take you off the usual tourist routes and share the insights and stories that you won't find in the standard visitor guides.

Ingleton has many claims to fame, but my personal favourite is one that would have saved me from numerous episodes of acute embarrassment.

Years ago, I travelled to the far west of Nepal to raft the gnarly Karnali. The river was so remote, we had to cross most of the country aboard a rickety bus. Then, we had to trek for two days through mountains and forest to reach the put-in, with sherpas carrying our rafts and over a week's worth of supplies.

When I landed in Kathmandu and met my fellow travellers, I discovered it was clearly an adventure with limited appeal to ladies. In a crew of twelve, I was the only female. I often thought we must have looked quite a sight when we stopped at the roadside for comfort breaks. A neat line of eleven blokes, with me squatting at the end with my skirt over my head.

But the Nepal trip was by no means the greatest loss of feminine dignity.

That honour belongs to my friend Anya, following an incident in the Brecon Beacons, near a mountain entertainingly called Fan y Big. Anya disappeared for ages, seeking privacy to answer a call of nature in the barren, treeless landscape. She returned looking very sheepish, and it took some time before she would 'fess up what had happened.

Famously, the West Indies wrote cricket calypsos to immortalise their victories with bat and ball. I felt Anya's triumph was worthy of poetic commemoration, although, being a serious person, I favour the limerick form:

A Moon with a View

Anya went for a pee up in Brecon
When something happened on which she didn't reckon
She'd just bared her arse
To squat in the grass
When Search and Rescue appeared doing recon.

Poor lass, she was caught in mid-flow
And that's the thing when you've just got to go
Once you've started, you must finish
Your golden stream won't diminish
Just 'cos a chopper's above flying low.

The comments rained down from on high
She accepted them all with a sigh
"Look, there's Fan y Big!"
Called the yellow whirlygig
A fact that no one could deny!

This advice you won't read in a book –
You could be caught by a bloody Chinook!
If you pause on a mountain
To create your own fountain
The RAF might drop in for a look!

That's the end of this sad tale of woe.
Airborne views of relief down below.
"Is it less bovver wiv a hover?"
We ask one anuvver...
Well, Anya would clearly say – "NO!"

As we arrived on the outskirts of Ingleton village, I saw a boundary sign that would make Hebden Bridge proud. It said, 'Ingleton: Home of the Shewee.'

The Shewee is a personal urination device which has freed women such as myself from the age-old nightmare of dropping their trousers to squat behind a bush, if there is one to be found, or braving the questionable hygiene of public loo seats.

Invented by Samantha Fountain in 1999 (there has to be a joke in there somewhere) the Shewee has enabled millions of women to relieve themselves while fully clothed and standing up, safe from the indignity of aerial ridicule from helicopters or other passing craft.

Investors on the BBC TV programme *Dragons' Den* rejected

Samantha's relief revolution, although others were quick to spot its potty potential. The product's website makes the heady claim that every three minutes around the world, a Shewee is sold. But it's not just for trekkers in Nepal or those dodging the Pee Patrol in the treeless upland landscapes of Brecon and Ingleton. The MOD (Ministry of Defence) ordered 20,000 of them so female soldiers would not be forced to compromise their modesty, or remove essential protective clothing in a war zone.

The power to pee. Women's liberation indeed!

While we're discussing urinary innovation, I must add that another now successful company called Captive Media also failed to secure funding on *Dragons' Den*. Captive Media's brainchild was the world's first urinal gaming system!

How does it work? The games respond to – well – the player's aim. Sensors in the pan link to an interactive screen above, which allows users to engage in hands-free gaming using what we can euphemistically call their own joystick. The game *On the Piste* requires a skier to knock over penguins, while *Clever Dick* is a true/false trivia quiz. Players accumulate points based on accuracy and timing, and can view their cumulative scores from successive bouts on Captive Media's website. They can even share their tinkling triumphs on social media.

I've always had slight penis envy, mostly because I would *love* to see how far I could pee up a wall. So, just imagine if these restroom revolutionaries teamed up! The Shewee and Captive Media are surely a match made in heaven, although I can't see it helping reduce queues for the ladies' loo...

I am a girl, but really. What do they do in there that takes so long?!

Mark was tired after our long drive the previous day. A late start and scorching heat made us decide against a long and shade-free ascent to the top of Ingleborough. Instead, we opted for a stroll down the hill to investigate the pretty village of Ingleton.

My second favourite of Ingleton's claims to fame relates to the eleven pale sandstone arches which stride majestically across the verdant green of the steep-sided valley, towering 80 ft (24 m) above the sparkling waters of the River Greta. Yet it is not the monumental magnificence of the structure that I love. It's the fact that its stones are imbued with a very British tale of stubborn and destructive rivalry.

Built in the 1850s, the 800 ft (240 m) viaduct was supposed to provide a critical link between two competing railway companies. The North Western Railway and the Midland Railway operated on either side of the viaduct, but like Tweedledum and Tweedledee, they couldn't agree to share the Midland Railway's Ingleton station. So, North Western built its own station outside the town, at the northern end of the viaduct.

The railway through Ingleton was destined to become the main line to Scotland. In the uniquely British tradition of putting the customer first, Midland and North Western were so unwilling to cooperate that they not only refused to connect the lines but also deliberately chose not to coordinate their timetables. This obliged passengers arriving at Ingleton station on one line to undertake a strenuous mile-long hike in all weathers, hauling their luggage down the Greta Gorge beneath the viaduct, then up the other side. Often while watching their onward connections depart.

Complaints mounted. In frustration, and to capitalise on the demand for rail services to Scotland, Midland proposed its own alternative, the Settle to Carlisle line.

North Western realised this would deprive it of its Scottish traffic, so eventually, the warring factions reached an agreement. But it was too late.

Parliament had intervened.

The government compelled Midland to build the Settle to Carlisle railway, even though by then, they no longer needed it. This neatly wiped the ready-made and more direct route through Ingleton straight off the main line map.

Midland's overarching, if hollow, victory didn't stop there. Prior to the 1920s, Britain had over a hundred individual rail companies. They competed fiercely, particularly where they bordered each other. However, the Railways Act of 1921 merged 120 of them into just four. The North Western and Midland Railways were lumped together with others to form LMS (London, Midland, and Scottish), the largest of 'The Big Four'. Despite being under the same umbrella, they continued their fight on the inside, although Midland usually prevailed. Its most visible victory was that the newly formed LMS adopted Midland's vibrant red Crimson Lake livery for all locomotives and rolling stock.

When we paused for lunch, we discovered that Ingleton's commitment to customer service didn't stop with its trains.

Since it was such a gorgeous sunny day, we found a café with outside seating, which overlooked the stunning vista of village, valley, and viaduct. There, a wonderfully rude waitress entertained us. She had appointed herself the ferocious guardian of an empty table, and kept moving her guests from table to table.

She greeted each new arrival to the café so politely.

"You can't sit there. I'm moving them onto that table." 'Them' being a couple midway through their lunch, who had to transport their own half-full plates!

"You can't sit there, 'cos that's a four to six. Oh. Are you going? You can sit over there, then..." on another identical table for four to six!

Some chairs were high chairs, so when a rather ample couple arrived, we awaited the showdown over the four to six, which was the only free table without stratospheric seats. Sadly, they opted for the high chairs and denied us the pleasure.

When we left, the controversial table for four to six was still empty.

Mark had a roast pork sandwich with apple sauce. It was huge and delicious and came with chips. I opted for carrot cake and a cuppa, as I didn't think I'd be able to hike after a roast pork butty. Looking at the size, I was right!

We meandered down to the start of the Ingleton Waterfalls Trail, one of the village's more mainstream claims to fame. At the gates, I launched into a hissy fit worthy of the waitress.

"I'm not paying £8 each to walk in the countryside. There's no shortage of walks around here for free!"

At £12 per person to explore the nearby White Scar Caves, tourist attractions are a swift way to burn through our budget.

The Pawsome Foursome had been so well behaved, wandering around Ingleton's independent shops on their leads, we treated them to their favourite thing: a splash in the river. They leapt from flat limestone shelves into deep pools, and swam in the cool water, stained amber by the moorland peat. We realised we were on the return leg of Ingleton's Waterfalls Trail, but we're not rebels! So we didn't continue up the trail unpaid and the wrong way round. There was a narrow section that led upwards through some rocks, but that wasn't the reason. I guess I'm just too conventional. Although my honesty and conformity didn't extend to averting my eyes when I had the opportunity to gaze upon a waterfall without paying the fee...

Back at the lay-by, we had a new neighbour. A dark blue van with yellow zebra stripes on the rear door, and a warning sign leaning up against its wheel.

It said, 'CAUTION. Cats Loose.'

The Fab Four were on their leads, since we'd crossed the main road, although there were no cats in evidence, other than Katt, the van's owner. A lady van lifer who travels under the moniker Wildkatt on the Road.

After the statutory Bingo call of, "Wow. Is that yours? That's a Beast!" Katt introduced herself.

"I'm a healer, shaman, and a drum therapist," she said. "I travel with four cats. These are my Savannahs." She brought out a pair of petite cats wearing miniature harnesses and leads. They were sleek and slender with beautiful leopard-spot markings. "This is Connie and Champion. The other two are my 'Ferals'. They wander free."

The Ferals were nowhere to be seen. Katt had a cat flap in her van so the Ferals could come and go at their leisure. As we got to know her, we realised Katt spent a lot of her time waiting patiently for them to return from their wanderings. It didn't seem to faze her. She used the time to create the fabulous hand-painted drums and other delightful art and craft items she sold on her website. She also bred Savannah cats because, "They are the perfect cats for van life. They're small, but ferocious and really good at guarding. Connie is my attack cat."

Katt asked us, "Do you mind if I interview you for my Vlog?" We agreed, and midway through the filming, a vintage motorhome pulled into the lay-by.

"Wow. Is that yours? It's a Beast!" the chap said as he descended from the cab. "I'm Bobby, and this is Linda. We bought this for a road trip around all of Britain, but it's a bit tame compared to yours!"

We finished the filming with Linda and Bobby looking on. Then, while Katt got down to editing, they came to look inside The Beast. They brought a bottle of plum wine and were surprised when we produced stemmed crystal glasses in our rough and utilitarian Beast.

When we started to travel full-time, I had just two red lines. The first was a fixed bed. When I'm tired, I want to go to bed, move directly to bed, and not start doing a jigsaw puzzle with cushions, sheets, pillows, and duvets. The second was that I refuse to eat or drink from plastic. I'd long since broken the Wedgewood dinner service we'd had to press into action because while cornering sharply, Mark dropped our everyday china out of the back of our van. The Wedgewood was a wedding present that had languished at the back of a cupboard for twenty years. Kept for best and never used – until we moved into a caravan! Surprisingly, my wine glasses had survived. I shared my special hack for transporting stemmed crystal ware, gleaned from five years of road tripping: slip them into a Bridgedale Merino Hiker sock and Bob's your uncle!

On depletion of the plum wine, our contribution was a bottle of Talisker Scotch whisky and suggestions for lesser-known highlights to visit in our adopted home county of Dorset. Linda and Bobby's little black fluffball, Neli, had joined us and The Fab Four in The Beast. He was gorgeous, and later, they introduced us to their Hereford mice, which were black with white faces.

We chortled at the realisation that between the three of us in the lay-by, we were travelling with five dogs, four cats, and two mice!

Later, when Katt showed us her video, she suggested we got in touch with her friend Paul, who ran the LorryLife Campers UK group on Facebook. At the time, we could not have known how useful this would be, or the opportunities it would present, particularly in the face of the coming storm...

Chapter 10

Ribblehead

The following morning, we made our push for the summit of Ingleborough. The culmination of my fifty-year wait to complete the Yorkshire Three Peaks Challenge.

The day was a scorcher, so we packed five litres of water in bottles and a Camelbak. Yet, only a third of the way up the peak's grassy limestone flank, cropped close by sheep and devoid of either shade or stream, we'd drunk the lot.

Our black and white boy, Kai, is not good in the heat. He flopped down behind the dry-stone walls in any bit of shadow he could find. He was clearly not enjoying our hike, and with no prospect of finding any more water, we abandoned our push to the summit.

Back at the truck, I wanted a shower, but that presented a variety of problems.

The first was that after almost three weeks on the road, our water tank was on the low side. That wasn't insurmountable. Katt had told us of another app called Nomad Services, which listed essentials like drinking water sources, Elsan points to empty chemical loos, and laundrettes. (At this stage, we didn't realise that Park4Night also lists such facilities.)

The second concerned our water heater not working correctly. It would not stay on, and kept making exploding, popping noises. We rang the company who supplied it, but the response was not good news. They diagnosed a cracked igniter, which sounded expensive and required a return to base. We were still learning the ropes, and didn't yet know the company's pessimistic tendency always to assume the worst.

Since they were back in Bournemouth, several hundred miles away, Mark spent the rest of the morning messing about under the sink to see what he could do. He tidied some wires; one trapped tightly behind a pipe. Personally, I wouldn't have thought releasing it made any difference, but the heater started working after that! Our park-up was also quite breezy. We wondered whether that was blowing out the pilot light, which would explain the re-igniting and popping sound. In any case, after that, we had hot water, so it was all good – apart from the next problem to solve: not having enough of it to take a shower.

"Do you want to go here?" Mark said as he interrogated his laptop for a plan of action.

"Where?" I asked.

"To the Ribblehead Viaduct?"

"HELL, YES!" I cried.

I was not sure I'd ever seen it. I must have done, since it sits beneath Whernside, the highest of the Yorkshire Three Peaks, which I had climbed with my dad. I can't believe my bridge-obsessed parent would have let the longest viaduct on the Settle to Carlisle line go unremarked, but I guess that aged 7, I was perhaps less awed by feats of Victorian engineering.

When we walked beneath it later, we met a man who said,

"My son saw the pyramids at Giza. He thinks this viaduct is even better than that!"

Yet, without the self-destructive idiocy of the railway companies described previously, the magnificent Ribblehead Viaduct would never have come into being.

Ribblehead is surely the crowning glory of the Settle to Carlisle railway line. Twenty-four stone arches, each over 100 ft (32 m) high, stretch a quarter of a mile (400 m) across a flat, beautiful, but desolate expanse of moorland called Batty Moss in the Ribble Valley. It both dwarfed and superseded the Ingleton Viaduct, which was completed with barely a broken fingernail. Sadly, Ribblehead claimed the lives of over a hundred of the 2,300 'navvies' (navigators) who built it. For the half decade it took to construct, they camped in ramshackle shanty towns around the site. Bear in mind that anywhere named 'moss' usually indicates a marshland. Conditions were gruelling, with challenging weather and difficult terrain, as well as outbreaks of fighting and disease. The church in Chapel le Dale has a memorial to the railway workers, and more than 200 graves belonging to some of the men, women, and children who did not survive the project.

We couldn't see any sign of the encampments, although the land surrounding the viaduct is a scheduled ancient monument because traces of their foundations remain. With dark humour, the workers gave the shanty towns ironic names such as Belgravia, Sebastopol, Jericho, and Batty Wife Hole. Belgravia, then and now, was a hugely affluent district of London. A world away from the cramped, muddy huts of the settlement. Sebastopol and Jericho were probably nods to the battlefield-like conditions on the construction site. One, a notorious siege in the Crimean War, the other, a biblical city besieged and reduced to rubble. As for Batty Wife Hole – it most likely refers to a nearby sinkhole or cave, although it's hard to imagine the men didn't relish the double entendre.

Like the navvies, we repaired to the Station Inn at Ribblehead, built at the same time as the viaduct to serve as both a pub and farm. The Station is still very welcoming. It has guest rooms named after the shanties that housed Ribblehead's labourers, and more importantly for us, a large car park that welcomed campers and provided both fresh water and waste disposal facilities. All available for free if you used the pub.

A former landlady, Vera Pitfield, who wrote about her time at The Station Inn in the 1970s, shed some light on the hardships railway workers must have endured a century before. Until the pub drilled its own borehole, it piped its water supply down from the fells. This dried up in summer and froze in winter, causing frequent water shortages. Vera recalls having to beg for, then collect her own water from neighbouring farms in five 50-gallon (190-litre) milk churns, which she stored in a back room. This strategy worked until the snows came – because then, even the snowplough sometimes got stuck!

Finally, I had my shower, and we dined in the pub that evening. For dinner, we enjoyed an epic home-cooked steak pie, brought to us by Leonardo DiCaprio. Well, at least he looked like the Hollywood actor, but he let slip that he was actually from Surrey. My pie came with a garnish of pretension. I mean pea shoots.

"Pea shoots!" I exclaimed to Mark. "On a pie? When did that happen in no-nonsense, plain-speaking, 'call a spade a shovel' Yorkshire?!"

Later, Leonardo inadvertently helped unravel this conundrum when we asked why he was so far from home in a rural pub in Yorkshire.

He said, "I came north to make some denarii."

For those who think Caesar is a salad, and are unfamiliar with ancient Roman coinage, that translates as, 'earn some cash'.

Because nothing says down-to-earth like slipping into Latin to say you're skint.

***

Sadly, allaying fears of a cracked igniter was not the end of our problems.

As we moved off from the lay-by, we noticed lumps of rubber falling off our chunky off-road tyres.

When we purchased The Beast, she was 30 years old, yet had fewer than 5,000 kilometres on the clock. Her mileage caused some issues with the Inland Revenue, who insisted that anything below 6,000 meant she was new, and therefore subject to Value Added Tax at twenty per cent. It took us months to convince them that since she came off the production line in 1990, she was actually old: a fact we now needed to come to terms with ourselves.

Her tyres looked pristine; they had only ever rolled 4,683 km. But sat out in all weathers for three decades, they had perished.

During the build, we had replaced all the hoses, gaskets, and other rubber components in the engine we thought might have degraded. Now, we clearly needed to replace the tyres.

We were sanguine about it. The new requirement that truck drive tyres must be fewer than ten years old would soon be law, so we would need to change those anyway. But tyres are fundamental to safety, and for Mark and me, that is non-negotiable.

Mindful of Ian and Willie's warnings about our split rim wheels, we made an appointment with a tyre shop in Preston which specialised in truck tyres.

"We have split rims," we warned them.

"That's no problem," they replied. "We deal with those every day."

So, you can understand why we set off to Preston with high hopes that we had everything in hand.

But nothing is ever that simple with The Beast...

Chapter 11

Wayward in Waddington

"Can I look inside your truck?" a chap with a pint in his hand demanded.

A classic Lorry Life Bingo quip.

He stood among the crowd that had spilled from the pub into the beer garden to bask in the July sunshine.

We were in the pleasant village of Waddington, where we and our Beast were causing somewhat of a stir.

Because we were trapped!

***

After a few days in a single location, it felt good to be back on the road. It had certainly been an 'interesting' onward drive from Ingleton across the Forest of Bowland. Our route followed a thin sliver of dark tarmac that took its time to unravel across a 312 square mile (803 sq km) National Landscape and Area of Outstanding Natural Beauty.

The Forest must be one of the least visited and most sparsely populated places in Britain. On such a fabulous summer day, the yellow moorland grasses contrasted sharply with the baby-blue sky. As with Hampshire's New Forest which is mostly heathland, the word 'forest' refers to somewhere with royal hunting rights, rather than the more modern meaning of a place covered with trees. As we rose, there were no trees in sight. The barren expanse of moor and moss granted us uninterrupted views back towards the full trio of Yorkshire's Three Peaks. Their unmistakable profiles jutted out belligerently from the horizon.

Near the summit of the Lythe Fell Road, we passed over a cattle grid so narrow, I wasn't sure we'd make it through. We had about an inch to spare on both sides. I winced and breathed in as Mark edged between the wooden posts that flanked us. His prowess earned a respectful salute from a group of black-leather-clad motorcyclists who'd stopped there to take in the view.

On top of the world, we pulled over for a cuppa at a snack van called Scrannies Brews and Bites. 'Scran' is northern dialect for 'food', while a 'brew' refers to a cup of tea.

Mark desperately needed a rest. We'd only driven ten miles (16 km), but the concentration demanded by the many twists, turns, and gear changes was exhausting. Despite being at an altitude of approximately 1,000 ft (305 m), the sweltering heat persuaded both dogs and humans to plonk themselves in the cool shade provided by our hulking Beast. Being so close to her, my anxiety ratcheted up as I noticed further cracks around the tyre treads, and a few more chunks of rubber that had parted company. Our trip to Preston was unquestionably the correct course of action. New tyres were an absolute priority.

The lady who ran Scrannies offered us some onward route advice. "There's a low bridge in Waddington, but if you turn left as you enter the village, you'll have no problems."

She was very impressed with The Beast, although I had mixed feelings about what she said next. "We have a Volvo tracked vehicle on our farm. It's bulletproof, but now we're struggling to get spares."

I just hoped it was many years older than our Beast.

***

Waddington.

Well.

As we entered the village, I looked up the left turn and glimpsed a yellow sign.

"Don't turn in!" I blurted urgently to Mark. "I think I saw a 'Road Closed' sign. It's really narrow, and we might be stuck if there's no room to U-turn."

In the village centre, we pulled alongside the Waddington Arms and called out to interrogate the afternoon drinkers thronging on the pub's lawn.

"Is that road closed?"

"Yup," came the answer. "But you'll be fine under the bridge down the road. It's 3.2 metres high."

"Um, we're 3.85 metres high, so no, we won't..."

"Artics from the quarry go under it all the time," he insisted. "You'll be fine."

"They might not be as tall as us."

"Course they are! You'll be fine."

As I said in Hebden Bridge, the public at large tends to underestimate our size.

We decided to proceed towards the bridge and check it out because our options, it seemed, were limited.

If we failed to pass through Waddington, we would have to re-trace our steps a significant distance back towards Ingleton. And if a *volte-face* was our only remaining option, we needed to find somewhere to execute said U-turn.

Near the bridge, a lady with white hair and a floral apron was tending flowers in the front garden of her gritstone cottage. As we approached, she shot upright in alarm. I think she thought there was an invasion coming. I leapt down from the cab to check the height of the bridge and reported back to Mark.

"It's not good news. It's definitely lower than us."

However, once the lady realised we were friends, not foes, she supplied better advice than our bibulous buddies at the pub. She indicated a tiny lane adjacent to her house. "Don't go down there," she said. "That's very narrow. But the road near the pub isn't closed until the end of the month, so you should be okay."

We turned around and pulled up alongside the pub once again. We had no choice but to obstruct a slip road, while Mark ran over to double-check who was telling the truth about the turn before we committed to it and got stuck.

The landlord came out and asked Mark, "Where are you going, mate?"

"Anywhere that will get me onto a main road!" he replied.

In the meantime, my chum with the pint engaged me through the cab window.

"I used to be in the military. Can I have a look inside?"

"Now's not really a good time..." I told him, mindful of the blockage we had created. Opening up the steps for guided tours outside a busy pub would neither facilitate a quick getaway, nor ease congestion on the village's already tight roads.

He fired the usual questions at me about The Beast, and I answered each one politely until Mark came back from checking our exits. Then, I performed the task that was becoming second nature – directing traffic as we reversed The Beast around narrow corners – while my friend continued his barrage regarding the mechanics of a Volvo N10 and persisted with his demands to see inside.

Flustered as I tried to direct Mark to reverse safely, without mowing down any of the pub's milling customers, or hitting any walls, buildings, or cars, I told him, "Normally, we'd love to show you the truck. But can't you see, now is *really* not a good time…"

As quickly as I could, I scrambled back into the cab. We drove off and restored peace and traffic flow to Waddington.

An indignant voice followed us up the road.

"Am I getting a look inside that or what?"

***

West Bradford Road was incredibly slender, with dry-stone walls along each side. A soft cushion of emerald-coloured moss coated each stone. Quietly, I mused, *well, it could provide* some *padding if we hit the sides…*

Even though The Beast was new to us, at least we had no reason to be precious about her faded, 30-year-old NATO green paint. We might have thought differently in a brand-new motorhome with shimmering, pristine paintwork, but a few scrapes and scratches would only add character to The Beast's muted, weathered patina.

The further we went, the narrower the lane became. Both of us felt a massive weight lift when we joined the main A59. In the long shadow of Pendle Hill, famous for its witches, we crept warily under a 13 ft

(4 m) railway bridge at Langho, but otherwise, sailed along the dual carriageway.

I'd found a pub stop by a canal near Wigan, but the turning we needed went almost back on itself. Once again, we pulled over to consider our options.

I called the pub to ask their thoughts on whether, "a large motorhome," which I described coyly as, "about the size of a lorry," would make it there.

"We get beer deliveries," the landlord answered. "Although it's a bit of a squeeze in the village with cars parked on either side."

I put it to Mark, but he shrugged.

I mean, how bad could it be?

We shuffled around the turn, and as we passed through the village, I could almost see into the upper-storey windows of the terraced houses that lined the streets. As with the cattle grid atop the Forest of Bowland, we had no more than an inch of clearance on each side between parked cars. I had to get down from the cab to guide Mark through. On one corner, a man rushed out of his house to move his car. If he hadn't, we wouldn't have got around the corner.

We had to make two sharp turns to enter the pub car park. By then, we had attracted quite an audience. Their faces all said the same thing. *You're not getting that in there...*

I worried when the publican ran out and shouted at me through my open window, although his warm smile soon allayed my concerns.

"Number one. I'm jealous!" he said.

"Number two, I won't mind if you go up on the grass a bit."

Mark skilfully avoided the grass and parked on the banks of the canal. As we jumped down from the cab, the bevy of onlookers all wanted a guided tour.

Our first guest made us doubt we would get a drink in this tavern.

It was only 5 p.m., but he was already swaying. We worried he might have drunk them dry!

"I live on a narrowboat on the far side of the bridge," he slurred, as he admired our surfboard-shaped mirror. The smooth varnished wood is very tactile, but I noticed his fingers immediately wandered up to trace around the nipple of the surf girl in the centre!

For those undeterred by the sticky floor, dated décor, and the sign on the door warning that 'Anyone suspected of using drugs here will be barred permanently,' the pub was a genuine hidden gem. The food was excellent, the staff friendly, and the location, right on the canal bank, gorgeous.

We had a couple of days to kill before our tyre appointment, so the next day, we relocated to another canal-side pub near the small town of Burscough.

"I'm sure this is where Ellie lives!" I said to Mark.

Eleanor is a friend from my London days. A fellow Lancashire lass, I was certain she'd moved back 'up north' to be closer to her family. I didn't know where, but a sign declaring 'Weight Limited Bridge in 250 Metres' took my mind off such musings. I weighed it up in line with the information coming in from the satnav and breathed a sigh of relief.

"It's okay, Mark. The satnav says we reach our destination in 210 metres."

Of course, it wasn't okay.

We found ourselves staring at a quaint pub with a packed outdoor terrace. It was on the opposite side of the canal, separated from us by a tiny lifting bridge with a 7.5 tonne limit.

So near, and yet so far!

Naturally, there was nowhere to turn around. Our only choice was to execute something like a 300-point turn, utilising as much of the canal's towpath as we dared, to the collective joy of the clientele enjoying the sunshine and the pub's canal-side location.

A lady dog walker told us, "You can get to the pub from the other side, through the industrial estate."

"Do you still want to stay here?" Mark asked, but by now, I really did.

The alternative route constricted in places, but was eminently do-able. Once we parked up in the pub's ample car park, we had the usual stream of visitors. A man with a broad Liverpudlian accent came over and gave our truck the ultimate Scouse compliment.

"Dat's boss, dat is!" he said.

As he ascended our steps, I noticed he had an electronic tag on his ankle.

"Are our phones still there?" I joked after he and his wife, who sported a fake tan, pneumatic lips, and a tight leopard skin print dress, had departed.

The heat was almost unbearable. We took The Pawsome Foursome for a much-needed leg stretch down the towpath. While ducks, moorhens, and fish appeared to thrive in the canal, the water's suspiciously opaque shade of khaki made me reluctant to allow our precious pups a cooling swim.

After so many pub stops, we felt somewhat replete with pies and pub grub, but the bar staff said a drink was fine to justify our overnight stay. This probably turned out for the best, since a family on the next table said they had already waited forty minutes for their food.

"We try to support our local pub, but every time we come here there's a problem," they told us.

They never got their food.

It took Mark twenty minutes to order drinks, and that was a process laced with irony.

Two teenagers staffed the bar. When Mark asked the barmaid, "What bitters do you have on?", she stared blankly and replied, "What's bitter?"

"It's... a type of beer..." he explained, doing his best to suppress laughter.

I'm surprised he controlled himself when she turned to her colleague and asked, "Do we have any beers?"

We decided on an early night, but sleep didn't come easily in the stifling heat. Even at 9 p.m., I was still dripping with sweat. The day just never cooled down.

**

The following morning, I awoke to a little voice outside saying, "All hail The Beast!"

It was a dawn raid with breakfast from Eleanor!

She said, "I got a message last night saying, 'I think we're near you', then realised Jackie Lambert, Mark, The Gang of Four and The Beast were half a mile away! It was too good an opportunity to miss an early morning coffee and pastry stop with my two gorgeous travelling friends."

She'd posted a photo of The Beast on social media, which already had a string of replies. When another friend, Neil, tagged me in a thread from a forum where I was not even a member, it became clear we were like a roving Where's Wally?!

Neil highlighted a picture someone had shared of our Beast captioned, 'Parked next to THIS!' The stream of comments followed a trend. 'I saw this on the M1', 'Do they have a load of cute dogs?' It seems our well-camouflaged Beast is anything but under the radar...

However, this lack of anonymity would soon prove highly useful.

Chapter 12

Trial by Trilex
Part I - Preston

Living the Dream comes in many forms, and for me, Friday 23rd July meant sitting beneath a tree on an industrial estate for three hours with four pups, trying to escape the searing summer heat.

In 1973, the Welsh rock band, Budgie, sang about being in the grip of a tyre fitter's hand.

Part of the soundtrack of my teenage years, I could never have guessed how prophetic this song would be one day, almost half a century on.

The Fab Four and I went for lunch while Mark oversaw getting our tyres changed. The café didn't allow dogs inside, so I leaned through the doorway and yelled out my order. With time to kill, I lingered over my egg butty at a red plastic table outside.

An hour later, back at the tyre depot, I expected everything to be done. As I handed Mark his sandwich, he said,

"We're having a bit of a problem..."

I experienced what was becoming an all too familiar Beast-related stab of trepidation.

"We haven't even got the first tyre off the rim."

The yard smelled of grease, rubber, and hot concrete. Other than a grubby white plastic garden chair in the dim and grimy Portakabin that served as an office, there was nowhere to sit and wait. The café was no longer an option. It closed at 2 p.m. and would have long since stowed away its red plastic seating assets. However, opposite the coffee shop, I had spotted a tree on the only patch of greenery to grace the grey industrial area.

My Kindle and laptop were both inside The Beast, which was up on a jack, so I had nothing to keep me occupied. I got strange looks from passing traffic. As working people came and went, they no doubt wondered why a middle-aged lady surrounded by four dogs would choose such a lovely, sunny day to perch uncomfortably on a postage stamp of grass at the entrance to a dour industrial estate, gazing into space.

Desperate times call for desperate measures. With more time to kill, and newfound skills with apps, I sorted out getting Facebook on my phone.

After I downloaded it and remembered my password, I noticed a few more replies on Eleanor's post about The Beast. One was very interesting.

Her friend, Simon, commented, *I used to hate changing those wheels!*

I pounced upon this flicker of salvation.

Simon had experience!

I didn't know him from Adam, but I seized the moment.

I duly dispatched a, "*You don't know me, but...*" message, and bless him, he sent through the mother lode of information. He explained that our Beast didn't just have split rims; she had Trilex split rims. While this elucidation was welcome and helpful, it only made things more complicated. Soon, we would learn that apparently nobody in the country, aside from Simon, possessed the vaguest clue what Trilex split rim wheels were, let alone how to change them.

Sometimes, the kindness of strangers really blows you away. On our behalf, Simon telephoned the tyre shop to explain the process of dismantling the wheel.

After long exchanges with Simon and Facebook, my mobile phone battery died. I returned to base at 4 p.m., convinced that everything would now be done.

Jubilant, I found The Beast sitting proudly back on six wheels, ready to go. My relief was short-lived, however, when Mark declared the sixth wheel was her spare.

Three sections of the wheel rim removed by the fitters lay scattered across the workshop floor. Mark said, "It took us hours to get the first tyre off. But then, they couldn't get the rim back together. Simon said we need a specially angled lever, around a metre long, to reassemble it."

Dave, the fitter, said he'd try to sort it the following day, which was a Saturday. We apologised profusely. The last thing anyone needs on a scorching Friday afternoon is a pair of truckin' idiots with a strange breed of wheel rim. We donated Dave a tenner to buy himself a well-deserved beer.

Mark and I repaired to a nearby pub for our own much-needed pint. Back in charge of my laptop, I pleaded for help on the LorryLife forum that Wildkatt mentioned.

By bedtime, I had about twenty responses and was becoming quite the expert on truck tyres.

At the last minute, almost as an afterthought, Simon fired across the advice, *It's important to torque the wheel nuts properly, and not with an air gun. If you get it wrong, when you brake hard, the rim keeps turning and rips off the valve.*

Mark revealed that Dave used an air gun (air impact wrench) to fit the spare wheel.

This was not comforting news and initiated a whole new bout of Beast-related angst.

Someone confirmed Willie's assertion that the trade calls split rim wheels 'widow makers' and explained the reason why. *If they're not fitted correctly, the metal rim can fly off with enough force to slice a person in half* they announced cheerily. So, that was why they needed to be inflated in a cage.

My cousin put me in touch with her best friend's husband, who ran a tyre fitting company in Carlisle. He told us, *I can give it a go*.

I didn't relish the sound of 'giving it a go' with a 'widow maker'.

When I sent over a photo of our wheels, he rapidly declined the job and declared *Those type of wheels are really dangerous*.

One helpful soul disclosed, *There's a military truck dealer on the B645 near Silverstone. I've seen trucks like yours outside, but I can't remember their name.*

I doubted anyone owned a truck like ours. The British army never used Volvo, and I'd only ever seen one other N10 in my life, and that was in Italy. 'It ' was worth a shot, but Google Maps didn't reveal anything resembling a military dealer on the B645 near Silverstone.

Some experienced overland truckers advised, *You need to change your wheel rims as soon as possible to a more conventional design.*

So, I emailed Volvo in Sweden.

The next day, we met Siobhan and Pete for the first time. I'd made their acquaintance on social media, and since they lived locally, they came over for lunch with their poodle, Rosie. They asked about our travel plans.

"We're in the grip of a tyre fitter's hand!" I said, quoting Budgie.

They looked confused, so I clarified, "We were on our way north to Scotland, but now, with no spare wheel, if we get a puncture and can't change the tyre, we're in real trouble.

"We bought a second spare with the truck because the *Haynes Build Your Own Overland Camper* manual said we should carry two. Many overlanders carry spare wheels on the cab roof rack, or on the back, but ours weighs over 100 kg. Because it's so heavy, the spare that is already on the truck has its own special mount with a winch system to raise and lower it. We have no way to lift such a heavy spare safely onto the roof or rear carrier. Plus, if it's mounted on the back, we wouldn't be able to open the rear barn doors.

"What I'm getting at is that our spare spare is in storage three hundred miles south, back where we came from in Bournemouth..."

After lunch, we tried to ring Dave for an update, only to find the tyre place now closed for the weekend.

So, our immediate travel plan was that we were stuck in Preston until we recovered our wheel on Monday.

The following week, Eleanor's friend, Simon, messaged to ask how we were getting on with our tyres.

Not too good! I replied. *They worked on them over the weekend but can't get the appropriate lever and couldn't fit the tyre. If we came to you, is there any chance you could help? If not, we will have to head 'home' to Bournemouth, as we have another spare wheel stored there. We're not too keen on touring without a spare, especially when seemingly no one in the UK knows how to change our tyres! I've emailed Volvo to ask whether we can change the wheel rims to something more mainstream. There's also a military base here in Preston, so we thought we might call in to see if they have a mechanic able to help.*

Simon replied to say that, although he lived not too far away, he no longer had the special lever or other equipment required to fit our tyres. When I spoke to them, the military base couldn't help either.

I'd spent the entire weekend looking for solutions, but was sliding into despondency. The optimistic certainty that 'There's always a solution' pulled us through the traumas, uncertainty, and looming homelessness we'd faced when we were building The Beast.

Now, all I saw was defeat.

I had contacted all kinds of plant and agricultural tyre fitters. Many raised my hopes by confirming they dealt with split rims all the time, until I admitted we had Trilex split rim wheels. Then, nobody had a clue.

I emailed the Shuttleworth Collection, a vintage aeroplane and motor museum with specialist engineers and mechanics at its disposal. I also posted on various military vehicle forums: *Trilex Split Wheel Rims in the UK – Help Needed! We have run into trouble trying to change the tyres on our Volvo N10, which has Trilex wheel rims – note these are not the normal split rims found on trucks and plant machinery.*

Then, I asked a friend who was a retired army engineer, and contacted the Tank Museum in Dorset.

All to no avail.

From Sweden, Volvo responded with characteristic efficiency, but said modifying the wheel type would be a complicated and technical feat that would involve new hubs and matching up bolt holes and rim sizes. They were unable to recommend anyone in Britain capable of changing our tyres, but mentioned that while Trilex was based in the Netherlands, they had a subsidiary near Loughborough in Leicestershire.

Clearly, we had an urgent need to add a Trilex tyre lever to our burgeoning supply of spares and rescue equipment. We trawled the internet, but there were none for sale. The dealer in Rotterdam who sold us the truck suggested they could possibly source one in a month or two, at a cost of around three hundred euros, but, post Brexit, we were well aware that importing it would be a fandangle of epic proportions. In desperation, we might have paid this extortionate cost, but we needed a solution immediately, not in a few months.

On YouTube, Mark found a video of someone separating and re-assembling a Trilex wheel rim with a bottle jack, while a friend from New Zealand sent a tutorial which showed someone blowing one apart using controlled explosions. I'm pleased to say that Simon advised us against both of these methods!

On Monday morning, we gathered up our bits of wheel hub from Dave and set our course south. Dave couldn't apologise enough, but we felt really guilty, too.

Despite ordering in expensive tyres for us, and spending many hot hours working on our wheel, he refused to charge a penny.

***

We routed ourselves back via Loughborough. There, Paul from Trilex's subsidiary looked in wonder at our wheels.

"I've never seen anything like that before," he said. "And I've never heard of Trilex wheels!"

He was very helpful, however, and agreed to contact the parent company.

Although he was on his way to the vet with his dog, he sent the information that afternoon. It made us feel better, even though it didn't help! Suddenly, we appreciated WHY Volvo fitted our truck with Trilex wheels.

The Trilex design is genius. The wheel rim splits into three, which enables an operator to change the tyre safely at the roadside with zero mechanical assistance. Instead of stretching a tyre around a rim, Trilex allows the three rim sections to be reassembled inside the tyre and levered into place. When re-inflated, the forces act inwards on the split rim, which avoids all of the widow-making risks.

How ironic that the perfect, no-fuss solution to switching tyres was causing us such a headache!

Our drive back to base in Bournemouth via Loughborough took two days. When we stayed overnight in a forest near Silverstone, we saw no sign of a military dealer there. However, our truck twin, Mike, who purchased his lorry at the same time as we did, posted a photo of The Beast on Facebook. His friend had spotted her while walking his dog in the woodland, and thought she might be of interest to his lorry-loving pal. Mike recognised The Beast straight away.

Once we'd recovered our second spare wheel, we breathed a little more easily, but we were all too aware it represented a mere stay of execution. Our retrieved spare would save us only once.

On a 15-tonne truck, the state of our tyres was a constant worry. Even without the looming rule changes, we desperately needed to find someone to change them.

By now, we had learned that Trilex was a popular system on the Continent and in Turkey, but we couldn't travel abroad to get our tyres changed. Britain remained locked down in the throes of the coronavirus pandemic, and there was no guessing when borders might reopen.

It was a ticking time bomb – and seemingly no one knew how to halt the countdown.

Chapter 13

Back to Base: Shake & Stir

W e were about as far south as it is possible to get without needing a passport.

Although it meant we'd missed Scotland by almost the entire length of the British Isles, I can't deny I was glad to be back in Bournemouth.

The Pawsome Foursome delighted in their return to the beach of their puppyhood. Kai was particularly playful and happy. It was a joy to watch his exuberance as he chased and splashed in the shallows. A stiff breeze from the ocean caressed my cheeks, while its salty fingers ruffled my hair. Although warm, it was still invigorating, and the soothing murmur of the surf seemed near enough the sound of home.

Yet something beyond familiarity made it feel good.

Besides reclaiming our spare wheel, our return to base offered an opportunity to get to grips with more of The Beast's outstanding issues.

Our electrics needed some attention. We'd bought 12-volt adapters to charge our laptops, but they seemed to overheat. The jack plug on Mark's melted, which didn't seem terribly safe or desirable on a piece of sensitive electronic equipment. We stopped using them and reverted to charging our computers from the inverter. This contraption converts the 12 volt DC (direct current) solar and battery power to 220 volt AC (alternating current) – equivalent to a mains supply. Long summer days and the heatwave meant no shortage of solar power, but inverting is wasteful, losing up to twenty per cent of the energy generated. We still had every confidence in our over-specified solar set up, but thought it wise to find a solution before the days shortened and we entered the period known to van lifers as The Season of Solar Anxiety.

Kellett Windows had sent some cowls to fit above the windows to stop rain coming in when we opened them, and finally, our blinds were ready. A friend agreed to receive these deliveries, so long as we promised faithfully not to turn up on her suburban doorstep in a truck.

Miles, the chap who helped with the conversion, noticed our Beast parked on the cliff top. He sent a text to say *I'm at Boss Vegas*, as he called Boscombe, a residential area along the coast. He offered the use of his yard, The Vision Vault, to work on The Beast. Fortunately, Miles had also kindly stored our van, Big Blue, there, so when we went to collect our parcels, we only needed to embarrass Helen with a mildly unconventional vehicle.

During our month on the road, the unfinished nature of The Beast had compelled us to embrace some rather eclectic rituals.

With no blinds on the windows, each night, we'd had to drape dog blankets over them to preserve our privacy.

Pilots use checklists to ensure they don't miss important procedures. In my flying days, the pre-landing downwind check BUM-FICH was my favourite:

Brakes off

Undercarriage down

Mixture – rich

Fuel & Flaps – on & sufficient

Instruments – set

Carb heat – on

Hatches & harness – secure.

It's always easier to remember a mnemonic if it sounds a bit rude. Some pilots FART on takeoff: **F**uel, **A**ltimeter, **R**adio, **T**ransponder, and others CRAPP on landing: **C**arb heat, **R**unway, **A**pproach, **P**rop pitch & **P**ermission to land.

In our caravan days, I carried this discipline through to a checklist for setting up and packing down. I still used **B**rakes off/on, **U**ndercarriage (jockey wheel and corner steadies) up/down, but added:

Toilet

Towing mirrors

Cables – electrical & breakaway

Reversing & other lights

ALKO stabiliser

Water pump – off, and

Locks – all doors secure.

Best of all, it spelled BUTTCRAWL – which made me happy.

As we did those hard yards with the caravan, we'd often looked on with envy as motorhomes and campervans arrived. They'd apply the handbrake, then be catching rays with a picnic thirty seconds later. On departure, following a leisurely breakfast or lunch, they would simply chuck their sun loungers in the back and drive off while we emptied, stowed, wound up, and hitched.

When weighed against a traditional camper, The Beast presented an additional layer of complexity. As you might imagine, her checklist differed from the caravan, but not in the way you'd expect.

The Beast had a few quirks.

Some were of our own making. Mark and I were married at a lighthouse in Scotland. After a ruthless downsize, most of our possessions were purely practical, such as clothing, cookware, crockery, and recovery equipment. Among the few fripperies we retained were two cast iron lighthouses, which looked nice by our door. One was just a generic red-striped doorstop. The other was a striking reproduction of the elegant black-and-white Cape Hatteras lighthouse in North Carolina, the USA's tallest. We also owned a headboard sliced from the bough of a 350-year-old hornbeam tree that grew in the grounds near our apartment. We had yet to work out how to fix these down permanently, and all were heavy enough to cause mayhem if they flew around as we drove.

Others constituted eccentricities left over from the construction.

We were still using Miles' stick and spring contraption to keep our kitchen drawers closed in transit.

Iain, our crazy electrician, didn't fit a switch on the water pump (or the fridge). The only way to stop the pump running dry if the tap accidentally opened while driving (and the only means to defrost the fridge) was to remove the fuse.

So, our pre-departure checks were Lighthouses – down, Headboard – off, Drawers – wedged, Fuse – out.

Disappointingly, I couldn't make that spell anything rude.

***

For some reason during our time at the yard, Miles was incredibly grumpy. Once, he switched off his angle grinder to yell at us because the dogs barked.

"T'farm next door milk t'cows at 4 a.m. and 4 p.m. They sleep in t'day."

It wasn't worth arguing about which noise was louder or more sustained: a dog bark, an angle grinder, or yelling.

Another time, I nearly died.

Mark reversed The Beast into its usual spot by the wall and killed the engine. Miles stomped out of his workshop and greeted us with, "You've touched t'ladder!" – a metal ladder behind the truck.

This kind of good morning is never a positive start to the day. During the long months of the build, Mark had endured Miles' Mercurial moods for more than a year. When I jumped out of the cab to guide him back, Mark's Milesometer had already hit 'seething'.

Stupidly, I got myself wedged between the wall, 15 tonnes of reversing lorry, and the ladder leaning on a heavy metal trailer. I shouted, "Stop," but an incendiary Mark, blazing with rage and impatience, was rushing the manoeuvre, and I was in his blind spot.

"Stop. STOOOOOOP!" I screeched.

But The Beast's engine roared, and swallowed my shouts whole.

I scrambled to climb over the ladder and trailer, but realised I had nowhere to go.

I was trapped.

Fortunately, the Vision Vault wasn't like space, and Miles heard me scream. He burst out of his workshop and intervened just in time to prevent me from being crushed. Shaking, I slunk off to hide, and make myself a restorative cup of tea. Later, I overheard Miles say to Mark, "I could hear t'fear in her voice."

I'm not surprised – I really thought my number was up.

I couldn't speak to Miles all day.

The truck had not even touched the ladder. My terror and shock soon curdled into fury that Miles had created such a stressful and dangerous situation for absolutely no reason.

Mark didn't improve my mood when he ticked me off.

"You should never get behind a reversing lorry."

After thirty-two years working in a transport hub, he knew that. Shocked and shaken, I had just learned the hard way. I didn't need a sanctimonious lecture on what a priceless idiot I was.

I needed a hug.

But every day's a school day.

In the aftermath of this incident, we bought walkie-talkies to facilitate clear communication over the engine noise.

They would be a game-changer.

***

At the very last minute, Miles invited us to Shake and Stir, a vintage festival. It took place at a park in Southbourne, another Bournemouth suburb. It seemed like a good deal. If we displayed our vehicle, we got to stay on the showground, Fisherman's Walk, for free.

Miles suggested we follow him there. When I saw him sitting in his van at the gate, I worried we had kept him waiting. With The Beast, hasty departures were a fantasy. Before she would even cough into life, we had to wait for her glow plugs to warm up and for air pressure to build in the brakes.

I knocked on his window and said, "We're ready to go."

He looked at me, bemused, and replied, "I'm just getting my van insured!"

He gave us directions to the festival. These were characteristically light on essential detail.

"Turn right at t'Co-op," he said, but when we got there, the right turn had two forks. Naturally, we chose the wrong one and found ourselves caught in the cyclone of Boscombe's one-way system in the Friday night rush hour.

That wasn't the end of our tribulations.

The park's entrance was narrow, with low branches, flanked by barriers at the perfect height to puncture a truck's fuel tank. An illegally parked car partially obscured the already constricted gateway.

An officious man in a high-visibility gilet wandered over.

"I spent twenty years directing lorries for the military," he announced.

A new square on our Lorry Life Bingo card.

Mark caught my eye and hissed, "Jax. I'm only listening to you."

The walkie-talkies were worth their weight in gold.

***

Our section of the display was host to a dozen magnificent vintage cars. The public thronged to admire gleaming chrome and rounded retro lines. Although there was a US military jeep, we were the only truck camper. From the moment the show opened, we had a queue of people who wanted to look inside. At lunchtime, I shut the door to stay the onslaught while I readied the pups for a comfort break. Undeterred, someone still climbed up the steps, rapped on the closed door, and asked to come in.

It was so busy on Saturday that I had no chance to announce our unexpected presence at the festival on social media.

On Sunday, I noticed friends outside, queuing for an audience with us! They were passing and happened to spot The Beast. I left

Mark hosting at the truck and rescued David and Clau from the line. I took them for a coffee and chat, away from the mayhem. When I returned, my foot had barely touched our bottom step when an indignant woman near the front of the queue pronounced, "Excuse me. EXCUSE ME! There *is* a queue, you know."

I turned to her and said, "This is MY truck!"

She didn't miss a beat.

"Oh well. That's alright then," she said, and indicated that I was free to proceed.

With a grin, I thanked her for granting me leave to enter my own vehicle!

Certainly, this was one of the show's highlights, but my absolute favourite interaction of the weekend occurred at almost the final moment. Last thing on Sunday, a lady brought a gaggle of teenage girls to view The Beast. She stood at the front and declared,

"You see, girls. There are different ways to live your life."

Ways other than encumbering yourself with the materialistic trappings of convention: mortgage, home, kids. Then squandering an entire lifetime slaving to pay it off.

What a lesson!

***

Her words made me stop and reflect. The path Mark and I have chosen is not just a way of living. It's a means to reclaim freedom in a society that tells you to anchor yourself with a house, mortgage, and possessions. Preferably ones you need to get in debt to afford.

Our lifestyle offers something different. It offers time. Time to explore, to think, to breathe. And time to be present in an existence that rushes by too quickly.

In a world obsessed with living longer, we rarely stop to ask if we're truly living at all. We pour our energy into routines that blur one day into the next: wake, work, eat, sleep, repeat. And in doing so, we sacrifice our 'Now' for a future that is never guaranteed.

Thankfully, Mark and I woke up to this. It took the sudden and unexpected deaths of two younger friends, then redundancy to force us to bring forward to today the hopes and dreams of our tomorrows. From our obsession with travel, we had already learned that happiness doesn't come from things; it comes from experience. And we'd observed that variety, and breaking out of everyday patterns, had the side effect of making time appear to slow down. Think how long a two-week holiday feels compared to a fortnight at work.

Waking up to the call of the sea, the swoosh of a forest, or the warmth of a summer sunrise makes you feel more alive in a single moment than in multiple weeks of tedious routine.

An obsession with longevity urges us to hoard time, clinging to it as though we could own it. But the lesson of a free life is that it's not the years or the possessions you accumulate that count. It's the richness of your days. Days filled with connection – to people, to nature, to excitement, challenge, and to yourself. Days when you're not rushing to tick boxes, but moving at the pace of your own curiosity.

Our lifestyle is not about rejecting responsibility or ambition. It's about prioritising joy and meaning. It's realising that the best way to honour time is not to stretch it out endlessly, but to savour it deeply.

The nugget of wisdom the lady instilled in her young entourage was that they had options and possibilities. They could explore and discover what was right for them and not let society and convention dictate that there is only one path worth walking.

They had the choice to live intentionally and step off the treadmill of expectation.

Instead of counting the years, they could count the sunsets and a myriad of small but fulfilling pleasures.

And then, they might find they had lived their lives more fully than most could dream.

Chapter 14

Trial by Trilex
Part II – Corby

O ur officious friend was there on Sunday evening to guide The Beast out of Fisherman's Walk.

He applied his full twenty years of experience in guiding trucks in the military and declared, "It's not going to come out!"

I begged to differ.

"It went in," I said, "so it must be able to come out!"

In the end, our exit was the exact opposite of childbirth.

It came out much more easily than it went in!

Our neighbour, in his sleek powder-blue and cream Lincoln Continental told us, "He directed me to go behind the lamppost!" A ploy that would have trapped him against a tree and ensured he had no room to manoeuvre his near 20 ft (6 m) length.

In the 1950s, the Lincoln was the most expensive car built in the US. It was Ford's answer to the Rolls-Royce Silver Cloud. New or old, it was certainly not a vehicle you'd want to scrape between a lamppost and a tree.

We were heading north again, since our mate, Rob the Roadie, had stumped up some invaluable information.

Rob had saved our skin a few times during the build. He'd sorted out our steps when the welder went AWOL, and along with Alex, stepped in when our erratic electrician, Iain, walked off the job just weeks before we became homeless.

After advising that we should have charged visitors at the show a £10 entry fee, £9.05 per photo, £2,500 per picture sitting in the driver's seat (double if Mark was involved) – and all subject to export tax and VAT, Rob made a suggestion that would change our lives.

"Why don't you contact Crouch Military about your tyres?"

When I looked them up, I found Crouch Military is an arm of a family-run company based in Kibworth, Leicestershire. Set up in 1948, they sell military vehicles, spares, and manage a huge international truck recovery operation. They are experts in their field. When we spoke, in a single sentence, Richard Crouch dispelled the long months of dead ends and despair with our Trilex wheels.

He said, "Call JB Rubber in Corby."

It would not be the last time Richard would step in as our saviour.

We called JB Rubber.

"Have you heard of Trilex wheels?"

"Yes."

"Do you know how to change them?"

"Yes."

"Do you have the appropriate lever?"

"Yes."

Those three affirmative answers sounded like the sweetest song of angels to our desolate ears, although, of course, in our lives, nothing ever goes completely to plan.

We departed for Corby, aiming for a pleasant park-up in Kingsclere, a Hampshire village famous for producing great racehorses.

Park House Stables, now run by TV presenter and national treasure, Clare Balding, trained the legendary Mill Reef. Named the fourth greatest racehorse of the 20th century, Mill Reef won races by lengths, not a piffling neck or a nose. In his debut race at Salisbury, he was six lengths clear of his nearest rival. Later in his first season, on a track turned into a mire by overnight rain, he won by ten lengths! *(A 'length' is the nose-to-tail measurement of the horse who crosses the line first.)*

As a child in the 1970s, I remember seeing Mill Reef with his front leg in plaster. He suffered a complex break on a training gallop; usually a death sentence to a racehorse. He underwent extensive surgery, which saved his life. His racing career was over, but at stud, he sired a string of winners.

But alas, Kingsclere it was not to be. The main A34 northbound was closed, forcing us onto the back roads. We left the M3 motorway near Winchester and filled up with cheap fuel at a supermarket. The shop was shut, but the cashier said we could stay overnight in the car park, since we wanted to stock up on supplies when it re-opened the following morning. She assured us, "There's no CCTV and no one checks," but we didn't feel comfortable. The spectre of a 3 a.m. alarm call from a security guard asking you to move on never makes for a restful night!

Park4Night listed the Winchester Park and Ride car park. It had oversized motorhome parking bays, but the signs said 'No Overnight Parking'.

At this early stage in our overlanding career, we were far too lily-livered to seize either of these golden tickets to a peaceful park up.

So, we pulled up behind an articulated lorry in a lay-by on the main road. Coverings for our condensation-prone roof lights remained an unsolved vagary of the build. All night, a streetlight glared down on us, while a relentless stream of trucks roared past. The pressure waves they created slammed into The Beast and shuddered through her frame.

Livin' the dream, people. Livin' the dream!

***

A few days later, we crunched onto JB Rubber's black cinder yard.

We'd spent the previous night at East Carlton Country Park, where we met Paula and her son. We were walking the dogs in the 102 acres of parkland that was once the grounds of East Carlton Hall. The impressive red brick and ironstone Hall was modified in the late 19th century in the style of a French chateau. It is privately owned, so it is not open to the public, but sadly stands empty and derelict, falling slowly into decline.

Paula lived locally and disclosed that the grand house there was haunted.

"I'm a nurse in a care home," she said. "A patient of mine worked at the Hall. She told me a ghostly woman used to stare out of the window."

This piqued our interest, and we discovered the Hall has its own 'Lavender Lady.' Back in the 1800s, East Carlton Hall was home to James and Ann, a wealthy couple who adored each other. Convinced lavender brought him luck, James planted it liberally around the house and grounds. Ann's most treasured possession was a red cloak James had made for her. She wore it constantly, and wouldn't let anyone else touch it.

When James fell gravely ill, he surrounded himself with lavender, but nothing helped, and sadly, he died. Grief-stricken Ann noticed an all-pervading scent of lavender. On Halloween, 31st October 1856, she climbed to the roof in her beloved cloak, calling James' name. A maid saw her too late. Ann jumped, and landed on a lavender bush below.

Ever since, people say her spirit still wanders the park, and if you catch an unexpected whiff of lavender... you may not be alone.

Spectres aside, East Carlton has some gentler claims to fame. It is one of around fifty 'Thankful Villages', those rare places where all its servicemen suffered zero casualties and returned safely from the First World War.

Still far too polite for our own good, we hadn't yet learned it's better to ask for forgiveness than permission. As a formality, we asked the park keeper if we could park overnight, assuming that staying in a large empty lot – where we couldn't possibly inconvenience anyone – would be fine. Naturally, he said, "No!"

He locked the gate of the gravel area where we'd positioned ourselves considerately to stay out of everyone's way, but the rest of the parking was unrestricted.

Polite we might be, but we're not very tolerant of stupid rules – an Achilles' heel that dogged our working lives. So we moved and set up by the bins... Another night livin' the dream – and another night where sleep was a joke.

Rosie had us up repeatedly with an upset tum, while the looming tyre debacle gnawed at our nerves. At 6.30 a.m., we were both wide awake. We knew our jobsworth park keeper would be back at 8 a.m., so to avoid confrontation, we slipped away quietly.

John, presumably the J in JB Rubber, greeted me with, "So, you'll be changing these tyres, then?!"

"I'm a northerner," I retorted. "I'm stronger than I look!"

"You know what they say about northerners," John said. "Strong of arm. Thick of head..."

John had the delivery and timing of a standup comedian. Who would have thought that getting your tyres changed in Corby could turn into an entertaining day out?!

In his gentle Liverpudlian accent, John gave a running commentary. He stood on the sidelines with a mug of tea while his chief fitter, Wayne, delivered a masterclass in tyre-changing on Trilex rims.

I filmed the process for our own benefit. However, since we'd had so much trouble finding information on Trilex, I uploaded it onto YouTube. JB Rubber shared it on their socials, and within a week, had over 1,000 hits. I am sure John's comical banter made a notable contribution to the rating.

John was so generous. He took time to show us techniques that would be invaluable 'in the field'. Although he had a machine to 'break the bead' (release the seal between the tyre and the rim), he asked Wayne to demonstrate how to do this manually, using a sledgehammer and a piece of angle iron. He allowed Mark to have a go at changing a tyre himself, then walked us through how to repair a puncture in the inner tube.

After all the hullabaloo about inflating tyres in cages, and one experienced overlander's judgement that Trilex wheels would be a huge problem, I timed Wayne both as he removed the rim from the tyre and as he reassembled it. With the correct tool and technique, each procedure took around 90 seconds.

After helping to change six of them, Mark said, "Now, I wouldn't swap our Trilex wheels for *anything*!" It was just so quick and straightforward. Like so many aspects of our truck, we would learn that Volvo engineering is unerringly robust, practical, and carefully thought through.

John sent us on our way with a puncture repair kit, his priceless Trilex lever, and an instruction to buy a 'Thin Wall 27' to torque our nuts. We couldn't thank him enough.

Despite sourcing nearly new military-grade tyres to keep the cost down, the bill for The Beast's pedicure was eye-watering. Approximately one-third of the price we originally paid for the truck! Maybe we should have heeded Rob's jocular advice and charged festival-goers for photos in the cab. One with Mark and one without would just have covered it.

On the bright side, we finally had a definitive answer to a classic Lorry Life Bingo question:

"How much does a tyre cost!"

John mercifully softened the blow to our retirement fund.

"There's a lot of weight in that. You don't want to be bumping up and down kerbs in it. But if you don't do anything stupid with them, those tyres will outlast you."

We treated ourselves to a trucker's breakfast in the industrial estate across the road, with a side order of a Thin Wall 27 from the tool shop next door. Mark and I rationalised the experience. Despite the stress, we were ultimately thankful for our Trial by Trilex.

"It happened here, in Britain, not in Outer Mongolia, and if we'd just snapped our fingers and got our tyres changed, we wouldn't have learned anything."

Now, we had more than an inkling of how to change a wheel, tyre, and repair punctures ourselves. It made us all the more self-reliant and able to rescue ourselves in an emergency.

I felt incredible lightness knowing that at last, The Beast's tyres were safe.

It left us with only one more thing to sort out.

Everything else!

Chapter 15

Foxton Locks

We hadn't expected to have the afternoon off, but since we had six new tyres and a full breakfast by 11 a.m., we repaired to the nearby Foxton Locks.

According to Google Maps, it had a huge car park and charged £3 for 24 hours. It was an outstanding stopover, with two pubs at the base of the locks, and two more within easy walking distance. In addition, it had public toilets, an Elsan point on the canal for emptying chemical toilets, plus footpaths and hiking galore.

Nestled in the rolling Leicestershire countryside, Foxton Locks is a remarkable historic site on Britain's canal network. It is England's largest flight of 'staircase' locks, which means that each lock opens into another lock. Foxton has two flights of five locks, with a passing pound in the middle and side ponds to act as reservoirs for the huge amounts of water required to fill and empty the locks.

Foxton is part of the Grand Union Canal, which, as its name suggests, came about from interconnecting many smaller canals. The link through Foxton, up a steep, 75 ft (23 m) escarpment, joined the Leicestershire and Northamptonshire with the Grand Junction Canal. Logistically, this was hugely important. It formed the first direct route for boat traffic between the East Midlands' coalfields and the River Thames in London.

We whiled away a sunny afternoon wandering along the picturesque towpaths and admiring the expansive countryside views from the whitewashed lock keeper's cottage at the top of the flight. The locks have changed little since they opened in August 1814, so we probably saw the same vistas as generations of boatmen and their families, who lived aboard and formed such a critical part of Britain's 18th and 19th century industrial transportation system.

The volunteers who staff the locks were keen to fill us in on the site's history. We discovered that between 1929 and 1947, George Durran was the lock keeper at Foxton. His duties included greasing and repairing the lock gates, cleaning the stables (the canal boats were horse-drawn), grass cutting, and tending the family's vegetable garden. All of which he managed perfectly, despite having only one leg and one eye!

These days, Top Lock Cottage is a shop, offering snacks and pre-loved books. George may well have traded there too; selling surplus home-grown produce to passing boats. He also supplied other essentials. The canal network formed a kind of 'linear village', so he would pass on vital news and messages between families and friends. Apparently, this 'Towpath Telegraph' remains an effective means of communication among canal dwellers today.

Like the railways, canals were privately owned and dug by navvies. Navvies worked long, hard days, and received payment by the cubic yard (slightly less than a cubic metre) of earth removed. They excavated around 12 cubic yards per day and earned about 30 shillings (£1.50) per week. This was three times the wage of a farm worker, although navvies had to pay all their own expenses, such as food, accommodation, and tools. However, some unscrupulous employers paid them not with cash, but with a 'Tommy Note', which they could only spend in company-run shops with inflated prices. Unlike the canal engineers, the real names of these workers are lost to history, but some of their nicknames live on. Characters such as Black Dave, Shakey Joe, and Northamptonshire Jack – each a tantalising hint of stories buried by time.

Narrowboats are a unique feature of British waterways. The constraints of early canal construction dictated their dimensions. A boat with a 7 ft (2.1 m) 'beam' (width) could carry 25 to 30 tonnes of cargo: a significant increase over the horse-drawn carts of the time. Thus, the builders deemed a 7 ft beam sufficient to transport a substantial load, while keeping the canal infrastructure – locks, tunnels and bridges – cost effective and simpler to construct. Locks were among the most expensive components to build. The slimmer gauge kept costs down, and narrow locks used less water; a vital resource, particularly on canals, which have no natural flow.

As the canal network expanded and interconnected, the 7 ft width became embedded to maintain compatibility.

Canal companies charged tolls according to the weight and nature of the load. They often permitted free carriage of manure out of cities: when you think of all the horses and the lack of sewer systems, this must have been a blessing to the urban population! Coal and stone attracted the next level of charges, with luxury items like pottery attracting the highest prices. Tollkeepers calculated their fees with a gauging rod. A barge sinks about one inch (2.5 cm) per tonne of freight. The rules stated that your dog was not allowed to worry a tollkeeper, so dogs were trained to stay on the boat. However, if you had pilfered some of your cargo, all hands and paws would stand on the same side as the toll keeper to make the boat appear heavier. If you wanted to measure light and reduce your tariff, everyone stood on the opposite edge, chatting the whole time to distract the tollkeeper. At Foxton, the toll office was in a part of what is now the Foxton Locks Inn, although to save money, the office closed in 1884 when tollkeeper, John Frisby Bentley, died.

We watched, fascinated, as colourfully decorated narrowboats ascended the locks. Like moving pieces of folk art, many sported the traditional hand-painted 'roses and castles' pattern. Synonymous with canal culture, 'roses and castles' relates to a type of decoration, rather than a specific illustration, although certain boatyards had their own signature style. The design includes vibrant motifs of red, pink, and yellow blooms, real or imaginary, intertwined with foliage. Alongside the flowers, pastoral scenes might depict fairytale castles nestled into idyllic landscapes, complete with winding rivers, romantic cottages, and distant hills.

The origin is unclear. Some believe it resembles the decoration on Romani gypsy caravans. The castles are certainly reminiscent of the mysterious fortresses we saw in Romania, where our caravan joined the mile-high club while crossing the Carpathian Mountains. However, experts have recognised echoes of German, Dutch, or Asian influences.

The designs often appear in panels along the boat's length, as well as on virtually everything else – including plant pots, jugs, fitted furniture, and even the horse's harness. Intricate geometric patterns or stripes border the panels, and their bold, cheerful colours stand out against a background of deep glossy green or black.

A floating gallery of canal tradition!

As with many itinerant communities, society looked down on the 'water gypsies'. They criticised their nomadic lifestyle, while paradoxically romanticising their colourful existence in literature and art. With a mix of genuine concern and patronising superiority, reformers such as George Smith of Coalville campaigned to 'civilise' canal families, and rescue them from their perceived lack of morals, manners, and refinement. The Victorians sneered at the roses and castles artwork, regarding it as vulgar, gaudy, and lowbrow, like the people. In contrast, the boaters saw it as self-expression, and a proud declaration of their culture, independence, and individuality – a sentiment we could relate to.

The Beast's interior certainly shared the same spirit – bold, bright, and gloriously unconcerned with fitting in.

Lately, the traditional style has seen a resurgence. Many owners choose to decorate their narrowboats with these vivid designs, and organisations such as The Canal and River Trust host workshops to teach the technique.

The boats' slow progress up the locks gave us plenty of time to admire the artwork, and even chat to the people on board. Each vessel took between 45 minutes and an hour to ascend or descend the entire flight of ten locks. Life on the waterways is unhurried, although we had to remain alert – and ensure Nosy Rosie didn't take the opportunity to hop on board and audit a slow-moving galley...

The two separate flights of locks provide some flexibility. It allows two vessels to travel the same way at staggered intervals. Plus, while a boat travels up or down on one flight, the second flight can be prepared to reverse. However, each flight has to complete its operation for craft travelling in a given direction before switching for the next set of boats.

Although Foxton Locks were hailed an engineering marvel when they were built, as canal traffic increased in the late nineteenth century, they became a bottleneck. Long queues were commonplace.

Engineer Gordon Cale Thompson provided an ingenious solution to this in 1900, when he completed his inclined plane boat lift at Fox-

ton. This groundbreaking mechanical system comprised two coun-
terbalanced water-filled tanks, each capable of carrying larger craft –
plus the water beneath them – up or down the 1:4 gradient hill. As one
tank descended, the other ascended. Gravity powered the lift, assisted
by a steam engine, whose boiler house is now the canal museum.

The lift transferred boats between the top and bottom locks in
twelve minutes; a vast saving of time and labour compared to navigating the locks. It could also handle two watercraft simultaneously
– one up and one down – as well as wider, more capacious barges.
This reduced delays even further and significantly increased the canal's
capacity.

The inclined plane earned a gold medal at the 1900 Paris Expo-
sition Universelle and was recognised at the St. Louis World Fair in
1904. These accolades underline and emphasise the lift's cutting-edge
design.

Unfortunately, despite its recognition as a technical wonder, its
operational life was brief. To justify its construction and running
costs, the lift demanded a huge increase in traffic. Just a year after its
completion, the Grand Junction Canal Company dropped its plans
for a lift at Watford and rebuilt Watford locks in their existing narrow
dimensions. This killed any hope of a 'wide' route to London, able to
accommodate bigger boats. The rise of the railways caused a decline in
canal transport, and the final death knell came when Foxton's inclined
plane required costly repairs in 1910. It was closed in 1911, and the
locks refurbished in its stead. The canal company kept the lift in
working order throughout the First World War, in case it was needed
for the war effort, but in 1928, they cut it up and sold it for scrap.

After being purchased for just £250, the plane exacted its revenge
on the man who took it away.

When Charlie Woodhouse loaded the metal onto his boat, it broke its back and sank.

In recognition of its significance in canal history, the inclined plane is now a scheduled ancient monument. The Foxton Inclined Plane Trust is spearheading its restoration. The long-term goal is the full reconstruction as a visitor attraction and piece of working heritage, but this will require substantial investment. All we could see from the viewing platform was a steep grassy bank with concrete footings for the rails. At the base, we found the large metal pulley wheel, which wound the steel cables. They recovered it from the canal's lower dock; possibly from where it sank with Charlie's boat.

We stopped for a pint at the delightfully quirky Bridge 61 pub at the bottom of the locks. It sits next to bridge 62, a turnover bridge also known as 'The Rainbow Bridge'. A turnover bridge enabled the horses towing canal boats to cross from one towpath to another without being detached from the towline. As for why it's called The Rainbow Bridge, I don't know. Its arched shape resembles a rainbow, but most canal bridges share a similar outline.

Canal memorabilia fills the pub's interior. Outside, its tables and garden overlook the still, reflective waters of the lower basin, where boats wait to ascend the locks. Historians think the pub building originally provided accommodation for workers on the inclined plane.

As usual, the dogs acted as icebreakers. Rosie sneaked off to greet the next table in customary fashion, wagging her tail, while eyeing up their snacks. Slyly patting them down for treats. The resulting apology started a lovely chat with a group of canal dwellers and volunteers. When they asked where we were staying and we told them about The Beast, the Towpath Telegraph proved its effectiveness. They all knew about the Volvo N10 camper in the long-stay car park! So much for stealth camping... They said they didn't mind us being there, and it prompted one chap to show us pictures of the magnificent vintage steamroller he'd restored. Another shared that he had travelled the world with his daughters, then sold up so they could benefit from their inheritance, while he lived a peaceful, contented, and minimal life on his canal boat.

I guess we all had one thing in common.

We were travelling folk and refugees from convention who had found our freedom – whether on wheels or water.

And like our forebears, we were all viewed as slightly suspicious by mainstream society.

Chapter 16

Lorry Lesson – Crouch Military

C rouch Military was expecting us when we announced ourselves at their gates at 8 a.m. sharp.

Not just because we had an appointment, or that they'd spotted The Beast making multiple passes before we found the correct entrance. Dave and his son, Richard, who greeted us, already knew that a Volvo N10 camper had parked at Foxton Locks. The Towpath Telegraph, it seemed, had stretched as far as Kibworth.

Given our lifestyle and plans, a regular Lorry Life Bingo demand was, "Are you mechanics?"

Since the detailed answer was, "No. In fact, we're as green as our truck!" we'd booked ourselves in with Crouch's foreman, Andy, for a lorry lesson.

We decided we may as well learn from the best.

Crouch Recovery has impressive credentials. They operate a fleet of over 150 heavy- and light recovery vehicles, including low loaders, mobile cranes, and winching units. You might recognise their signature orange livery, and perhaps not only from spotting them on the road.

The company featured in the UK TV documentary series, *Trucking Hell*.

Andy directed us into a maintenance bay. Painted white and sparkling clean, it was more like an operating theatre than a workshop for heavy machinery. He guided Mark and The Beast onto shimmering stainless steel tracks. At the push of a button, our pride and joy rose in front of us as if on a giant dentist's chair. There was no crawling into dark, oily pits here. With our home elevated above, Andy walked us through our list of questions.

He gave us a tour of the ten-litre mechanical mystery that lay under our bonnet and helped us decipher the rubber spaghetti he revealed. "I'd take photos of all these belts," he advised, "so you have a record of how and where they are fitted when you come to change them."

Then, with a pencil-thin torch as a spotlight, he took us beneath the chassis. His illuminated expedition brought to light grease nipples we didn't know we had, and highlighted the axles and prop shaft which had so captivated Ian Coates and Willie. I chuckled at the thought of discovering their legs sticking out from under The Beast at Bridestones.

A couple of hours later, once we were done, Andy introduced King Kosh. The newest member of Crouch's fleet was undergoing restoration in the adjacent bay. This mighty Oshkosh 8-wheel-drive monster had a winch on the front and a crane on the back. The Oshkosh is US-built to undertake *very* heavy-duty recovery; think of tanks or armoured vehicles on challenging terrain in battle conditions .

We considered our Beast a titan, but King Kosh dwarfed her. Drenched in a lustrous coat of Crouch's blazing burnt orange, The King's pugnacious bull nose and square-jawed radiator grille exuded authority. Behind the cab, twin chrome exhaust stacks gleamed. We peeked into the cab's luxurious interior, lined with sumptuous cream leather. It was a killer addition to the Crouch fleet and a great advertisement. This machine didn't just command attention; it demanded it.

Andy handed us over to Richard, who treated us to a look around Crouch Military's storage shed. Inside was a collection of rare historic vehicles that would have made most museums jealous. It smelled of musty canvas, engine oil, and age. I gazed in wonder at a dusty split-screen Austin, an ancient military ambulance, and the full evolutionary arc of Land Rovers through the ages. There was even an elderly recovery truck, painted in Crouch's colours. It looked like it dated from the early days of the company, which Richard's grandfather founded in 1948.

Richard explained, "We moved into collecting military vehicles because we bought them to convert into recovery vehicles in the '60s and 70s. These days, we buy, sell, and restore for collectors and enthusiasts all over the world." Outside, a beautiful dark green flatbed with a rounded snub nose was manoeuvring around the yard. "We hire some of them out to the film and TV industry. That old Bedford has just been filming at Pinewood Studios."

We thanked Richard profusely for sharing his treasures with us and dragged ourselves away from the truck porn. We would be back in a few weeks for a service, to prepare The Beast for her MOT test, which was due at the end of September.

Andy dispatched us with an inventory of ongoing maintenance tasks and recommended spares for our trip. He'd even looked up all the part numbers and noted them down for us!

This was the start of a love affair with Crouch's. One of those fabulous companies who are old-fashioned in the sense of providing service way beyond the call of duty.

As we drove out, Mark declared, "We need to get organised and draw up a proper maintenance schedule. I can see how important it is to keep our nipples greased, our balls polished, and our flanges lubricated."

But somewhere between the axle chat, the grease-streaked tour, and King Kosh's gleaming chrome pipes, something had shifted.

For the first time, we felt a little less like impostors behind our oversized steering wheel. After a morning exploring The Beast under Andy's watchful eye, we weren't just fumbling passengers anymore.

We left with slightly more knowledge and the quiet satisfaction that we were growing into our overalls.

No, we weren't mechanics.

We were not even close.

But we were starting to feel marginally less green than our truck.

Chapter 17

Remember, Remember the 5th of November: Stoke Dry

B ack at JB Rubber, John had mocked us when we said, "We're on a tour of the UK."

"And you came to Corby!" He guffawed.

True, the industrial town of Corby isn't renowned for its tourist industry, but I maintain that wherever you go, you will always find something of interest.

First though, let's get one thing straight. The famous fact you *think* you know about Corby is completely wrong. We should iron out this pressing concern by deploying the town's alternative motto:

Corby. Nothing To Do With The Frikkin' Corby Trouser Press!

That curious contraption, which lurks in the corner of seemingly every hotel room in the world, wasn't born in Corby at all. Instead, it hails from Windsor. Its name comes not from the town, but from its inventor, Peter Corby, an RAF veteran. In the passionate pursuit of banishing creases in a gentleman's lower trouser, Corby (the man) created what is surely among the world's most ubiquitous but niche products.

Yet, despite its omnipresence, I still don't know anyone who has used one – except when they got back late from a business meeting and deployed it to reheat panini.

Which brings to mind comedian George Egg, the Snack Hacker.

He took Corby Cookery to a level way beyond rolling up a leftover pizza slice to create a Corby Calzone. On tour, he came up with his own creative solution to bland and expensive hotel food. At a demonstration in Bournemouth, he whipped up a three-course meal using only a trouser press and a steam iron.

However, I digress.

Back to actual facts about Corby, which will astound you even more than a chef who can conjure a gourmet spread from hotel valeting equipment.

Corby's nickname, 'Little Scotland' might sound like a stretch for a town in Northamptonshire, just 72 miles (116 km) north of London. Still, this place, almost 300 miles (483 km) distant from Alba's southern border, sells more Irn-Bru per capita than most Scottish towns. (Alongside Scotch whisky, many consider the bright orange soft drink to be Scotland's other national beverage.)

Corby is also home to one of the world's biggest Glasgow Rangers fan clubs.

Numerous towns have local football rivalries; think Manchester United and Manchester City, or Liverpool and Everton. Yet, in Corby, the tartan truth is that lively competition is more likely to feature fans of Glasgow clubs Rangers and Celtic. And *hoots mon*! The local accent has an unmistakable Scottish lilt. Corby even holds its own annual Highland Gathering, filled with bagpipes, Highland flings, and muscular men tossing their cabers.

So, how come this peculiar slice of Caledonia came to be plonked in the English Midlands?

Two thousand years ago, the Romans mined and smelted iron in the area. Thirteen hundred years ago, the earliest recorded settlement took the name of an 8th century Danish Viking chieftain, Kori. Then, in 1086, the Domesday Book mentions a place called Corbei (Kori's By, meaning Kori's Settlement. Corbe is also the Old French word for a crow or raven, which features in the town's emblem.)

Fast forward nearly a millennium, and Corby's iron ore deposits attracted a Glasgow steel tube manufacturer, Stewarts & Lloyds.

In the 1930s, they built one of the UK's largest steelworks in Corby. In the midst of a depression, tens of thousands of unemployed workers from Glasgow and Aberdeen migrated to Corby, a village numbering about 1,500 residents. This twentieth-century influx led to such expansion that, in the 1950s, The Town and Country Planning Association declared Corby, population 18,000, a 'new town'. The 1961 census revealed that a third of Corby's residents were born in Scotland.

Which helps to explain another curious fact about Corby.

The town is twinned with Châtellerault in France, Velbert in Germany, and Shijiazhuang in China, but it also has a more cosmic connection.

The town gave its name to a crater on Mars!

Corby's unexpected extraterrestrial interconnection began with a freakish twist of history that involved porridge and a rocket.

Corby's Highland Gathering includes a porridge eating competition, which, in a blast of interstellar oatmeal, came to the attention of NASA's Apollo 11 space mission. When they discovered a 4.1-mile (6.6 km) crater on Mars in the late 1970s, they named it Corby. The reason is down to a conversation held between Michael Collins, Apollo 11's Command Module Pilot, and Bruce McCandless from NASA Mission Control. In 1969, McCandless shared important world news with the crew. This included the earth-shattering revelation that in Corby, England, Irishman John Coyle had won the World Porridge Eating Championship by consuming 23 bowls in 10 minutes.

Without dropping an ear of zero gravity cereal, Collins replied that he would like to enter Buzz Aldrin, because, "He's already on his 19th bowl. Over."

***

We eschewed Corby's tartan-tinted charm and post-war industrial architecture and opted to park a little way out of town, albeit in a place that still had steely connections. Herein lies the charm of Corby – it is close to a lot of lovely stuff, including Britain's smallest county.

Rutland is known for its historic market towns, built from honey-hued stone with either thatched or local Collyweston 'slate' (limestone) roofs. I first encountered Rutland's 18-by-15-mile (29 x 24 km) resplendence over thirty years ago. A friend of mine, Paul, was a Raddleman, as Rutlanders are called, born and bred. The noble intention behind my visit was in connection with a special operation. My selfless act of service was to help drink his dad's pub dry because the lease had ended.

Needless to say, my recollections of that trip are hazy, although I can relay that while there, my participation in a drinking game taught me an important life lesson.

The winner of each round had the dubious honour of choosing the ingredients for the next forfeit. When my turn came, with an entire bar to choose from, I cackled as I dreamt up the vilest cocktail imaginable. My masterpiece, a toxic-looking concoction of Blue Curaçao and a random assortment of horrors, oozed with the treacly thickness, iridescent sheen, and suspiciously dark, opaque hue of crude oil. I smirked and clasped my hands like a cartoon villain, already savouring the grimaces of revulsion drinking it would inspire.

Of course, I lost the next game and was forced to consume my own horrific creation. You could say I had tapped my own keg and drowned in the foam...

But it goes to show; you should never wish ill on others, in case karma serves it straight back at you, on the rocks.

My visit also enlightened me to a curious chapter of the county's history.

Paul told me, "In 1974, disaster struck in Rutland."

It seemed that a nationwide reorganisation of local government meant Rutland lost its status as an independent county. Its bigger neighbour, Leicestershire, swallowed it up.

Outraged, the people of Rutland launched a spirited campaign to regain their independence and prevent faceless ledger-wielding overlords from erasing a proud history and identity that had been theirs for thousands of years.

As part of the 1990s resistance, Paul said, "We all still use our old postcodes, and keep replacing the Rutland boundary signs."

Locals certainly embraced their motto, *Multum in Parvo* – Much in Little.

The turning point came in 1997, a couple of years after my visit. Finally, the people made their voices heard, and their insistence that their pint-sized county deserved its place on the map bore fruit. April

1st was Independence Day – when the government officially reinstated Rutland as an independent county.

Rutland may be small, but it proved it could take on the bureaucratic behemoth and win.

In Rutland, size doesn't matter.

But self-determination does.

***

A swift investigation of Google brought to light a rural park-up just over Rutland's hard-won border, on the banks of the Eyebrook Reservoir. Built in 1939 to supply Corby's industry with water, Eyebrook is minuscule compared to its sister, Rutland Water. They created Britain's (and one of Europe's) largest man-made lakes in the 1970s to quench Corby's steelworks' ever-increasing thirst. These days, both reservoirs are nature reserves. Previously, Mark and I visited Rutland Water to windsurf, but were disappointed to find that hardly any of its 23-mile (37 km) circumference welcomes free-running pooches like ours.

We parked near the tiny hamlet of Stoke Dry, in a lay-by with beautiful views over the reservoir. Considering its proximity to such a large expanse of liquid, it seemed a little mis-named. Although the lake is relatively recent, at one time, the valley floor was marshland, so the fourteen houses on a hill above were indeed dry. And may have been even drier when the marsh was drained.

Nature treated us to a lilac sunset, which contrasted perfectly with the rolling golden landscape of wheat fields and the scatter of ancient stone dwellings. Flocks of waterfowl fluttering and chattering on the shoreline and the occasional bleat from sheep grazing peacefully were all that broke the silence. Yet, when we walked The Fab Four through the fragrant summer evening, we found it hadn't always been that way. Not only that, Eyebrook had a surprising connection with a place we'd once visited by accident on our travels.

A passing rambler revealed, "This is where they practised Operation Chastise. You know, the Dambusters raid, with Barnes Wallis' bouncing bomb?"

A few years earlier, during another quest for prime windsurfing, Mark and I ventured to Edersee in Germany. We hadn't connected the dots, so it shocked us when the tourist office started talking about the dam. Only then did we realise that Edersee was home to the Eder Dam, one of the Dambusters' three objectives. The thought that someone might assume we were there to gawp at a place where Allied bombing led to 1,600 civilian fatalities made us deeply uncomfortable. I had nothing but admiration for the bravery of the crews; it was an audacious, potentially suicidal mission. The site holds undeniable historical significance, but being there was a humbling reminder that in war, the price of victory is paid too frequently in the blood of the innocent.

Eyebrook's size, shape, and proximity to RAF Scampton, home to Guy Gibson's famous 'Dambusters' 617 Squadron, was ideal for simulating the conditions of the raid. I found it hard to imagine the roar of four Rolls Royce Merlin engines as massive Lancaster Bombers skimmed the water at the suicidal altitude of just 60 ft (18 m). To put this in context, the Avro Lancaster's fuselage is 69 ft (21 m) long and its wingspan 102 ft (31 m). This gave precious little margin to avoid catching a wing tip when making sharp turns, such as the manoeuvre required once each plane had released its payload at Edersee. Failure to bank sharply meant the crew of seven faced certain death by crashing into the mountain straight ahead.

The man also told us about the village's remarkable St. Andrew's Church.

"Its murals and friezes are really rare. Most medieval artworks in English churches were destroyed or painted over during the Reformation – you know, when the Protestants broke away from the Catholics in the 1500s. The church still has its original Norman and Saxon stone carvings. One is the earliest known depiction of a bell ringer in England! There's a painting that shows the death of St. Edmund. He's tied to a tree and shot with arrows. The Danes killed him, but the bowmen are wearing feathered headdresses, so some historians think they are Native Americans – drawn centuries before Columbus discovered the Americas!"

When I researched it later, I found that Edmund, King of East Anglia, did fight the Vikings. When they captured him in 869, he refused to renounce Christ, so the wonderfully named Ivar the Boneless murdered him. Ivar had Edmund lashed to a tree, shot with arrows, and then beheaded, just to make sure.

Eventually, Edmund's followers built a rich shrine and abbey in Bury St. Edmunds, and elevated the martyred King Edmund to patron saint of England. Unfortunately, from the Middle East to Middle England, a dragon-slaying upstart called George from Cappadocia in Turkey, who wasn't a knight at all, and never even visited Britain, usurped Edmund in 1350.

In patron saint terms, Edmund was downgraded to pandemics. This came about when King Louis VIII of France fled from a failed attempt to invade England in 1217. He pinched some of Edmund's remains from the shrine at Bury and interred them in Toulouse. Four centuries later, the populace made the perfectly reasonable assumption that some relics (they weren't sure whose, but subsequently plumped for Edmund's) saved the city from plague.

Yet George endures as one of Christianity's most popular saints. St. George is venerated in cities and regions in Spain, Italy, Greece, and various other parts of Europe and the Middle East. He's very much in demand as a patron saint. England shares him with Georgia (obviously), Russia, Bulgaria, Portugal, Lithuania, Ethiopia, Malta, and Serbia.

Besides its saintly shenanigans, we also found that the church had an intriguing connection with the Gunpowder Plot of 1605. This was when Guy Fawkes famously tried to blow up the House of Lords during the state opening of Parliament. The scheme was a Catholic rebellion, designed to assassinate King James I, and wipe out the Protestant establishment in a single, catastrophic blow. Once they had created a power vacuum, the conspirators intended to install a Catholic monarch, James's young daughter, Princess Elizabeth. Under their influence, of course. Had the plot succeeded, it would have changed the course of British history.

Sir Everard Digby, a wealthy Catholic gentleman, played a significant role in the operation. He funded it and was planning an uprising in the Midlands once the conspirators had enacted the plot. Digby owned Stoke Dry Manor, which is near the church. Local legend suggests that, under the guise of attending a religious meeting, Digby, and his collaborators may have gathered in the small chamber above the porch of St. Andrew's.

Although Digby fled when the plot failed, he was captured and held in the Tower of London. There, he was tried and executed in 1606. Specific evidence tying Digby's actions directly to the church is sparse. His ownership of the manor is a firm association to the village, and the secluded rural location certainly lends itself to secrecy. While we will never know the exact details, it links the tiny village of Stoke Dry with one of the most infamous events in British history; an incident which is still celebrated today.

Each November 5th, Guy Fawkes Night, also called Bonfire Night and Fireworks Night, continues to take place all over Britain to commemorate the foiling of the plot. It originated because Londoners lit bonfires to celebrate the king's survival. As a child, I remember the rather gruesome tradition of creating an effigy known as a 'Guy' to burn on the fire – although both Fawkes and Digby's executions for high treason were by hanging, drawing, and quartering. Allegedly, Fawkes, an old soldier, jumped off the scaffold and broke his neck, which spared him the rest of his agonising sentence.

An Act of Parliament enacted in 1606 required the population to attend a service each November 5th to give thanks for sparing the king. The Act was repealed in 1859.

Which simply goes to show that on this unexpected road trip we'd embarked upon, wonder is all around. You just have to look.

Even in a village with 35 residents, and the new-but-old industrial town of Corby!

Chapter 18

Truckin'
Disasters & A
Walk in the Park
– Mappleton

A
t times, I feel blighted.

Things had seemed to be going so swimmingly.

We left Stoke Dry early to visit the Burrough Hill Fort, a striking and well-preserved Iron Age hillfort. The earthworks comprise a ditch and rampart. They crown an isolated ironstone promontory, which grants the fortress commanding views for miles over the low expanse of the Leicestershire countryside.

Ancient sites captivate me. Just standing on the remains of such places gives me a buzz. It doesn't happen everywhere, and I can't predict where it will, but some locations instil in me a profound sense of connection with generations of ancestors who walked the same ground. As the sun and wind caress my face, I can almost feel echoes of the past. It bridges time and brings to life the aura of those whose lives were shaped by the same changeless elements. Ordinary folk, who had hopes and dreams, and may well have gazed out upon the same horizon.

At Burrough Hill Fort, I experienced this incredibly strongly. The earth beneath my feet felt alive with history; although with every other step, the squeak that had developed in my right trainer detracted somewhat from the powerful ambience.

The car park prohibited overnight parking, so we had planned to move on after our walk. However, when the landowner arrived and saw The Beast, he voluntarily offered permission to stay. He even asked, "Do you want me to turn on the water so you can fill up?"

Our beautiful truck does seem to bring out the best in people!

I loved staying in such a wonderfully atmospheric place, although I didn't sleep well. The following morning, I had to admit to Mark,

"I dreamed we ran out of funds and I ate a puffin!"

The next day of livin' the dream involved a trip to a large out-of-town shopping centre in Loughborough. Our objectives: pet food, truck parts – and footwear.

My life couldn't continue with one squeaky shoe!

As yet, we still had to solve the conundrum of the MOT-defying broken windscreen wash bottle, as well as the various fan belts needed as spares.

I had the relevant part numbers, and thus far, I had found our wash bottle on the Volvo Penta marine website, which wouldn't let me order it. I'd emailed Swedish Truck Parts in Rochdale, Charles Trent Motor Salvage, and Truck Parts Online, none of whom could help. Bison Parts yielded a glimmer of hope. They could supply spares for a later model, the Volvo F10, but not the N10. Volvo Parts stocked components for cars only, and GCP in Sweden specialised in classic Volvo car parts. But even if they had what we wanted, post Brexit, it would be nigh on impossible to import.

But on the upside, we had six new tyres and understood our Trilex wheels.

Unsurprisingly, Loughborough's motoring and hardware chain stores were light on replacement rubber gear for elderly lorries.

On our way north, I spotted a Volvo truck repair centre. I phoned to ask whether they could supply the wash bottle and other spare parts we required. Even with the part numbers, they couldn't. They recommended Digraph for aftermarket lorry spares, so I rang them. The wash bottle was a 'no', but Nicky did her best to find the fan belts we required, although they were not listed. She said she would email some pictures to see if we could pick out what we needed. Then, we called into a company nearby who manufacture grease nipples. As soon as we arrived, a man came out to marvel at The Beast, and break the news, "Sorry, mate. We send them straight to our packing plant. I love your truck, though! When I was a kid, I restored a Land Rover someone dug out of a field."

Our ultimate destination was a pub in Derbyshire, just outside the Peak District National Park. It was an ill-advised choice for several reasons, only one of which was immediately obvious.

The road leading to the village sported a sign that declared it 'Unsuitable for Coaches or Caravans'. Of course, Mark simply viewed this as a challenge.

"It doesn't mention lorries!" he said as he turned the wheel and passed the point of no return.

Our satnav, which has The Beast's dimensions and weight programmed in, was unperturbed by our choice of route. For me, the drive down the narrow, winding lane qualified as 'interesting', but despite the ban, I was certain that I could have driven Big Blue and Caravan Kismet down there with zero issues. As we pulled up in the pub car park, it appeared that another couple had been equally unperturbed by the sign. Ali and John were enjoying coffee and sunshine from their magnificent blue-and-white converted coach!

They popped over to say, "Hi", so we invited them to look in The Beast. Then, they showed us around their bespoke bus.

"It started life as a recycling bus," they said, "so we made the interior from all kinds of upcycled and repurposed materials."

They had done a wonderful job. Inside, everything was beautifully crafted and individual. I particularly liked the innovative use of old varnished circuit boards as a wall covering.

They loved the polychromatic intensity of The Beast's playful colour scheme and paid us the huge compliment, "She's the loveliest conversion we've ever seen."

Although considerably more neutral, their bus was exquisite.

The pub food was delicious. My slow-baked pork belly with black pudding and apple-flavoured gravy was melt-in-the-mouth gorgeous.

The young lass behind the bar was a sweetie. She told us, "I'm going straight from a 12-hour shift in the pub to Leeds Festival to see Liam Gallagher from the band Oasis. The gates open at 3 a.m."

Oh, to be young again, and able to burn the candle at both ends.

Mark and I both felt weary, and with no phone signal or internet, we party animals enjoyed a cup of mint tea and an early night! We contributed a generous tip to help towards her festival costs, despite her giving us another table's bill... Fortunately, we noticed dinner was a tad expensive, and received a £17 refund!

Since we were still in the midst of a heatwave, we got up with the larks the next morning to do the longest of the three walks from the pub marked on the map they gave us.

This one led through Thorpe village, and up Thorpe Cloud, a striking limestone cone, which rises sharply behind the village, at the entrance to Dovedale. The place names derive from Old English: *Clud*, means 'hill', and *Dæl*, 'valley'.

We had a brief look around the strange little church, St. Mary's, in Mappleton. An incongruous Italianate dome supporting an octagonal belfry tops the squat, square tower fronting the tiny stone oblong. The church's curious mix of styles arose from its reconstruction on the foundations of an older building, though its true claim to fame lies in *who* built it. Nobody knows how James Gibbs, pupil of Sir Christopher Wren (of St. Paul's Cathedral fame), came to design the teensy place of worship in the mini-village of Mappleton-in-the-Middle-of-Nowhere. Gibbs, of course, was behind the slightly famous church of St. Martin-in-the-Fields in Trafalgar Square, and St. Bartholomew's Hospital in London.

In the cool morning air, the pups charged through the rolling apple-green fields. They leapt through the narrow gaps that nicked through grey lichen-mottled dry-stone walls to serve as stiles. It wasn't until we encountered a field of bullocks that we realised the second reason why our trip to the Peaks was ill-advised, although again, it was not the reason you might think.

As we made to squeeze our way through the stone stile into their field, the bullocks rushed towards us. I kept the pups back – I had heard tales about herds of cows attacking humans with dogs. I wasn't sure what to do, but Mark decided to try his hand at bull whispering.

Mark has a way with animals. My favourite memory is of a tiny foal who clambered up on top of his walking boots to get near to him. His little hooves were slipping off Mark's toe caps, but the foal just wrapped itself around Mark, then followed him to the furthest boundary of his field like a lovesick puppy.

I took a photo of Mark with the bullocks gathered around him in a semicircle. It looked as if he was telling them a story. Another shot captured him rubbing an enraptured white calf behind the ears, and yet another shows a blue marl baby stretching its neck towards Mark's face, as if to plonk a smacker on his chin.

But as swiftly as they came, the bullocks turned and wandered away. I crossed safely into the field with The Fab Four, impressed by Mark's zoological communication skills.

That was when the explanation became clear.

I saw a farmer at the far end of the field, his pickup loaded with sacks of feed.

It wasn't Mark's animal magnetism that had attracted the bullocks; it was a case of mistaken identity. They thought he'd brought breakfast!

When we caught up with the farmer and commented on his happily munching bullocks, he said, "They're Holsteins crossed with Belgian Blues. They're much easier to manage than Friesians. They are nasty!"

It was then that we discovered the second reason our destination was ill-advised.

The farmer said, "I'd avoid Dovedale if I were you, *with it being the bank holiday.*"

In our drifting, nomadic bubble, the clocks and calendars that govern most people's lives have little hold on us. The outside world's obsession with dates and deadlines is no longer a concern. Which is why we were blissfully unaware that we had chosen a sunny August bank holiday weekend to tackle a walk voted one of Britain's Top 100 – in the busiest part of a national park!

The first clue came when we joined the human conga inching toward the summit of Thorpe Cloud. It felt like we'd hit rush hour on Everest's famously gridlocked Hillary Step.

As we approached Dovedale itself, an unending swarm of day-trippers spilled from the adjacent National Trust car park and obscured the famous stepping stones across the River Dove. We arrived from the peace of the open countryside, where – crucially – there was no sign that said 'Dogs On Leads'.

Although she is part Poodle – a water retriever – our little black minx, Lani, is normally reluctant to get her paws wet. The one exception she makes, however, is for ducks.

Once, we lost her for forty-five minutes in Italy's Lake Garda. She set out to pursue a small flock, serenely ignoring our frantic calls. Each time she got too close, the ducks simply lifted off and landed just out of reach. As she doggedly swam after them she gathered an amused crowd, and at one point, we genuinely thought we might have to dive in to retrieve her.

So, when Lani spotted ducks standing in the shallows, instinct took over. Without warning, she bolted upstream, scattering wildfowl like the bow wave of the Titanic. We called – or maybe bellowed – her name, but in such moments she develops selective deafness. Once she'd cleared the area of anything feathered, she turned back to acknowledge our summons with an angelic *Who? Me?* expression that was worthy of an Oscar. Unfortunately, our yells had drawn the collective gaze of everyone within earshot. A ripple of tuts, huffs, and mutters about irresponsible dog owners spread through the crowd as it elbowed its way up the picture-perfect dale.

Even without Lani's attempt to lose friends and alienate people, one look at the chaos was enough.

As Lani trotted ahead, radiating self-satisfaction, we beat a hasty retreat back to solitude, where following the herd is strictly reserved for animals grazing on the hills.

Somehow, in a field near the much more tranquil Thorpe village,

Rosie lost her collar. At Thorpe's Norman church of St. Leonard's, we met a lovely group of National Trust walkers. One lady described her trip to Nepal just before lockdown. Then, a gentleman called Jim filled us in on a few intriguing features of the church, which explained how England's longbow archers became such a formidable force in battle.

"St. Leonard's dates back to 1100. See that sundial near the porch? It was not for the plebs. It's really high, so it was only visible if you were on horseback. You can also see grooves in the stone on either side of the church door, caused by people sharpening their arrows! Back in the day, by law, all men between the ages of 15 and 60 had to practise archery every Sunday after church. Playing football or dice games was banned because it was a distraction from archery. They often kept the archery butts in churchyards."

Medieval Europe really feared the massed English longbowmen. All those years of practice from boyhood gave them devastating power. Archaeologists have found archers' skeletons with massively over-developed bones in their arms and shoulders – all from using longbows. Their bows had a draw strength of 150 pounds and could fire accurately over 250 yards (230 m) – or even further just to harry the enemy. Each archer could loose 12 arrows per minute – far faster than a crossbow – and their arrows could pierce chain-mail and plate armour.

No wonder they obliterated much larger French forces at the pivotal battles of Crécy, Poitiers, and Agincourt.

Mounted knights, once the terror of the medieval battlefield, could be cut down long before they got anywhere near the English lines.

In our former life, Mark and I used to practise field archery. The draw strength of my bow was 28 pounds. I have fired a 40-pound bow, which our instructor told us was a common draw strength for medieval women. I managed it, rather shakily, once or twice, and brought up a lovely bruise when I twanged my forearm with the bowstring.

I simply cannot imagine the strength required to draw a 150-pound bow twelve times a minute for the duration of a battle.

Jim also told us, "I'm 82. I lost my wife 18 months ago, but I still get out and about."

Mark and I were heartbroken for him. Yet we always say, 'You get the face you deserve' – and Jim was the epitome of this. He really didn't look his age, and afterwards, Mark said of the entire group, "Those are all glass-half-full people. It was such a pleasure to meet them."

Unbeknownst to us, it wouldn't be the last we'd see of them.

When we got back to the pub to treat ourselves to a post-walk pie and a pint, they were all there having lunch. Then the following day, when we walked to Ashbourne, a fine old Derbyshire market town, we met Jim again. He was outside the Queen Elizabeth's Grammar School building, which was founded in 1585 by Britain's first Queen Beth.

He rather pooh-poohed the measly five-mile walk he did with the National Trust the day before and said, "I'm doing a 10-miler today. I walk 36 miles a week!" He also told us, "I used to have my own business. I was a glass and crystal worker. I was just admiring the windows in the school here. You can tell the original Elizabethan glass because the panes go straight into the stone mullions, with no wood or lead."

Our third walk, through the gorgeous Okeover Park, didn't end well.

We got slightly lost, and although it was a sunny bank holiday, we saw hardly a soul as we crossed into neighbouring Staffordshire, and enjoyed the grounds of Okeover Hall. The manor has been privately owned by the Okeover family since the Middle Ages, so it is not open to the public. The stunted ancient oak and chestnut trees that studded the parkland particularly captured my attention. Rounded, irregular burrs adorned their thick, gnarled, and twisted trunks. They had a magical, otherworldly appearance, and reminded me of the Whomping Willow in the Harry Potter films. An abandoned farmhouse, built from golden stone and surrounded by all this beauty, even made Mark and me spend a moment contemplating moving back 'in the brick' and settling down in one place.

Back at the pub, we thought about our life choices even more when we realised another impossible quest had just landed in our laps.

A jagged scar stretched across the front of our truck, catching the light like a fragile spider's web might catch the morning sun.

"Someone has cracked The Beast's windscreen," Mark said, incredulous.

There was a kiddies' playground at our end of the car park, and it looked like somebody had thrown a stick or stone, then scarpered.

Ever the optimist, I said, "They can repair cracks up to about three or four inches long."

"But it looks longer than that," Mark replied, "and it's at the edge of the screen, so it's much more likely to fail in an accident. We won't be passing an MOT with that."

Deliberate or accidental, we stared at it and felt utterly defeated.

Here we were, faced with another rare, irreplaceable part on our burgeoning list of hard-to-find spares and items vital to MOT success.

So, for our next trick, we had to conjure up a replacement windscreen for a 30-year-old truck.

Chapter 19

Carsington – What Can You Do in 15 Minutes with Glass Polish & a Piece of String?

M ark and I repaired to the pub to drown our sorrows.

My unshakeable belief that 'There's always a solution' struggled to cope with this latest hurdle. Plus, it offended my sense of justice. I believe in treating people properly, which includes taking responsibility for your actions and the impact they have on others. Unfortunately, it means I expect too much and am often disappointed. But for eighteen months, we'd poured our souls and our sanity into building The Beast. Someone had damaged her – broken her windscreen – and simply walked away.

It seemed like a personal affront.

I felt embarrassed as tears welled up, so I pushed my head into Mark's shoulder and tried to swallow my sobs.

"How can somebody do that? They've left us with a vehicle that is potentially illegal to drive, tricky to sort out, and probably a hefty bill. Two people on a forum I follow said it took them four months to get a replacement windscreen for a normal German motorhome. Not a vintage Swedish lorry. And that was before Brexit."

Britain had left the EU (European Union) the previous January. From the difficulty we'd had getting certain items we needed for the build, we knew only too well the impact of Brexit on the cost and availability of components sourced from the EU.

"Our MOT is due in a few weeks. We won't pass with a broken windscreen. What are we going to do if we can't drive the truck for months on end? It's bank holiday. Nowhere is open. And we don't even have internet here to look for a solution."

The landlady kindly invited us to stay another night. We didn't hold her responsible, but the breakage had definitely happened while we were there. She said she would ensure that in future, campers parked further away from the kiddie play area.

When you're drowning, you can either give in, and let the waters swirl you off on a wave of self-pity, or make a desperate grab for anything that will keep you afloat. Since we had no internet or phone signal, we did the only thing we could. I dried my tears, took a deep breath, and signed into the pub Wi-Fi to research truck windscreens.

Clearly, we would be stuck for a while until we got the screen replaced, so we found a campsite nearby, and moved the following morning. It was more field than camping ground and close to Carsington Water. Unlike Rutland Water, at least Carsington offered dog-friendly walks.

Farmer Paul's expression when we arrived suggested I'd done the right thing when I'd euphemistically told him to expect, "A large motorhome," rather than a truck.

He visited after we'd settled in. Once he got over the initial shock, he became rather taken with The Beast. He told us, "I farm 175 acres on my own, so I only get one week's holiday per year! I love Bournemouth, though. We often go there for our holidays."

He said his kids love crabbing, so I suggested Mudeford, a beautiful place – and a prime spot for catching crabs.

A flock of children staying on the campsite came to look at The Beast, and a few rode in the cab while we positioned ourselves on top of the hill. Then, we got down to the serious business of organising a windscreen replacement.

With a fresh bout of positivity, I remarked that, "At least we hadn't stuck our Crit'Air sticker to the windscreen that got broken, so we don't need to get another one!"

Crit'Air is France's emissions-based vehicle classification and is a necessity for driving in certain low-emission zones. It's not expensive. The sticker costs only a few euros and lasts the lifetime of the vehicle. The problem is, it takes several weeks to arrive and is complicated to receive when you're a nomad with no delivery address!

Hours of fruitless research on the internet soon made me feel rather less positive, however. I queried specialist windscreen businesses, all of whom came back in the negative. Bereft of ideas, I said to Mark, "I suppose we should really contact our insurers. After all, they will foot the bill."

Like most insurance companies, they used Autoglass for windscreen replacements. We had zero confidence in the ability of a mainstream car glass company to handle the requirements of a 30-year-old truck, but as instructed by the insurer, Mark dutifully spoke to them.

It was Bank Holiday Monday.

When he came off the phone, he said, "They are coming to fit the windscreen on Thursday."

I couldn't hide my disbelief. "What? You did tell them we needed a screen for a 1990 Volvo lorry?"

"I did, and they said they have one in stock. They seemed pretty confident."

I might have snorted in derision.

"I'll believe *that* when I see it..."

***

So, let's go through the true saga of what happened when Thursday came.

10:07 – Having successfully located 'The big green army truck in a field near Carsington', The Cavalry (Tyrone and John) had arrived and were ready to roll.

10:16 – They had prised out the old windscreen, placed a fresh rubber gasket around the new screen, with string inserted into the non-glass side of the gasket to drag it into place.

10:17 – It was in!

10:20 – They gave our new screen a bit of a polish and were done.

***

I truly hadn't believed that was going to happen! We'd spoken to

Autoglass on Bank Holiday Monday, and within three days, they'd found and fitted a windscreen to a vintage truck. Apparently, the screen is listed on their database. I was in awe.

I thought it would be difficult to source the glass. When they got it so quickly, I was convinced it definitely would not fit. If it did, I imagined it would take hours to install – but once again, Volvo's practicality and fitness for field repairs shone through.

It was five stars from me!

I had offered the guys a cup of tea. They said no, probably because they knew the kettle would not have boiled in the time they took to replace our screen.

As they packed up, Tyrone told me, "We're part of Autoglass Specials Division. We get asked to do all sorts. I changed the glass on Chitty Chitty Bang Bang! They kept me on standby the whole time they were filming. Light reflected off its windshield, so depending on the shot, we had to keep putting it in and taking it out. It was fun working on the set. The food was incredible. They had a French chef doing the catering. Someone asked for a burger, and he was furious. He said, 'I don't do burger!' It was all marinated lamb shanks in red wine."

Tyrone assured me that the broken screen wouldn't have shattered. "It's laminated, so it wouldn't splinter. Most people don't change them until it's time for their MOT."

Like the tyres, the windscreen was not something we were prepared to leave to chance, but with our MOT due, the replacement was certainly timely.

We'd made a step in the right direction, but until we sourced a windscreen wash bottle, we knew we wouldn't pass.

In the meantime, however, our next challenge was to convince the Italian government we were worthy of a long-stay visa.

Chapter 20

(Don't) Miss Marple

W hen it came into force, Brexit hadn't just mucked up our ability to buy goods from the EU. It meant Britons had relinquished their right to live, work, and travel freely for however long they wanted in the Schengen visa-free zone. That placed most of Britain's doorstep within the bounds of the world's most unfriendly region for long-term travellers.

It was because of Brexit we'd bought The Beast.

Denied a stay longer than 90 days in every rolling 180-day period in most of our home continent, we needed a Brexit-busting plan.

Brexit prompted me to utter the phrase, "Let's go to Mongolia," to my beloved, which set in motion a whole sequence of events. Since our caravan was unlikely to survive such a journey on the rough roads of Central Asia, we bought a 24.5-tonne, 6x4-wheel-drive ex-army truck blind off the internet and converted her into a self-sufficient off-grid tiny-home-on-wheels.

As anyone would.

But a couple of factors had conspired to put Mongolia off the cards for the moment.

Minor details, such as the route being closed due to a global pandemic.

That sort of thing.

Most of Europe had reopened its borders for intra-Schengen travel but implemented strict requirements for travellers from non-Schengen areas, which, of course, included post-Brexit Britain.

Not to be outdone by having access denied to its citizens, the UK only permitted journeys abroad to an ever-changing 'green list' of countries, with mandatory hotel quarantine imposed on anyone returning should the lights change to red during their stay. At a cost of £1,750 per person to self-isolate for 10 days in a government-sanctioned hotel, it was a powerful deterrent.

Even if we could have got through Europe, COVID-19-related border closures, quarantine, and entry restrictions put in place by most nations along the route rendered our journey to Mongolia impossible.

We needed a Brexit-busting Plan B.

With the reduction in cases of COVID-19 during the warmer summer season, coupled with the removal of most domestic rules, such as mandatory mask wearing and social distancing, we dared to hope. Were a few months skiing in Italy a possibility? Where we'd been able to stay for the full six-month season in the past, we thought Brexit limited our options to 90 days.

Until we met Those Weirdos.

Those Weirdos, as they called themselves, were a dreadlocked and pink-haired couple with a child, two rescue dogs, and a cat. They lived in a bright yellow, long-wheelbase Mercedes Sprinter, and they had a plan.

When we encountered them in Wantage, they were on their way to

Portugal.

For less than the cost of a second-hand car, they had bought a plot of ground, where they intended to park their van and live sustainably off-grid.

A liberty Britain's restrictive planning laws will not permit on your own land.

When we asked, "How can you do that after Brexit put the kibosh on freedom of movement?" they introduced us to the wonder known as the Schengen D Visa.

A Schengen D Visa lets non-EU citizens stay over 90 days in the issuing nation and still use their 90-day Schengen travel allowance elsewhere. Each country has its own application criteria and will only grant visas for specific purposes, such as study, work, family reunification, or long-term residence. However, some countries offer a D Visa for tourist reasons, or for digital nomads. It was a stretch, but I was certainly a nomad and used a laptop, which was digital. As an author and blogger, my efforts don't provide me with anything approaching a living, but I thought maybe the cap might fit...

The availability and ease of obtaining a D Visa varies depending on both the applicant's country of origin and the nation to which they request entry. As Those Weirdos found, some countries, such as Portugal, were more straightforward. Others, like Norway, were not even worth considering.

You must usually apply for visas in your home country, either at the nation's consulate or through an outsourced application centre, for example VFS Global.

Some initial research into Italy's criteria is why you now join us livin' the dream in a car park in the Metropolitan Borough of Stockport, Greater Manchester.

Although we were back in my part of The North, which I associate with friendliness, Marple gave us a mixed reception. Our interactions deviated from the customary, 'Wow! You're living my fantasy life,' or Lorry Life Bingo witticisms concerning The Beast's fuel economy.

Sharp tones of outrage shattered the morning's peace.

From bed, we overheard a man speaking loudly on his mobile phone. Mark peered out through a slit in the blinds, worried he might be reporting us.

"There's a manky monstrosity in the middle of the car park!" The man fumed.

"A manky monstrosity!" Mark whispered with quiet rage. "How dare he call The Beast a manky monstrosity when he's in a knackered old Skoda!"

As we descended the steps to take The Pawsome Foursome for their early morning essentials, a lady squinted at us and asked, "Are you a breast screening unit?"

I didn't have to kick Mark. He is a gentleman.

So, he didn't reply, "It could be arranged..."

Our park-up was next to Marple station, from where we could catch direct trains into the centre of Manchester. We had to submit our Italian visa application through VFS Global, which has offices in London, Edinburgh, and Manchester. With four dogs and a large truck, we figured Manchester might be easier than central London.

For a functional stop, the car park wasn't too bad.

Marple itself is a small town which exudes quiet elegance and understated charm. It nestles amid leafy trails and rolling hills, right on the doorstep of the Peak District. A local artist, Eric Jackson, perhaps irreverently, called Marple 'The jewel of the Cheshire Alps' and noted that Marple has 'only one road in and one road out' – although like Ingleton, it does have two train stations.

It seems incongruous for somewhere so bucolic to be part of industrialised Stockport, whose smoking factory chimneys inspired artist L.S. Lowry's urban landscapes.

However, before Greater Manchester swallowed Marple in 1974, it was in Derbyshire, then Chehire. Far more appropriate bedfellows than dark satanic Stockport, you might assume.

We were next to Brabyns Park. Historically, the 90-acre area of woodland and open parkland, bordered by the River Goyt, was the estate of Brabyns Hall. In the still relentless heat, The Fab Four dived straight into deep shady pools in the river, whose winding path we followed as it snaked its way between tall trees and sheer sandstone cliffs.

Sadly, Brabyns Hall no longer exists. The opulent Georgian mansion, built in 1749, was demolished in 1953 as part of what was recognised too late as a nationwide cultural tragedy.

After WWII, Britain lost countless grand houses. During the war, the government requisitioned them as military headquarters, training facilities, barracks, or hospitals, then returned them in a poor state of repair. Post-war, a shortage of staff made running these labour-intensive estates a challenge. Society was also changing. The survivors of two world wars shunned a life of servitude to the upper classes and sought better wages elsewhere. Then, a hike in 'Death Duties' to pay the colossal cost of the war forced the aristocracy to offload their cash-guzzling ancestral piles. Some pre-emptively demolished them to reduce the financial burden, particularly when inheritance taxes would prevent their heirs from keeping them anyway.

At that time, historic houses had no protection in law. Focused on rebuilding after having their lives disrupted by war, the populace saw them as relics of a bygone era. Rather than part of our national history, they stood as symbols of outdated aristocratic privilege and inequality. So much so that the demolitions were often public spectacles, watched as entertainment.

So, between 1945 and 1974, over 600 noble residences were torn down. In 1955, demolition erased the country's architectural heritage at a rate of one great house every five days. Estimates suggest Britain lost one in six historic mansions and country houses.

Another local casualty in this wave of destruction was Marple Hall, built in 1658 by Henry Bradshaw III.

Just a few years before the hall was built, John Bradshaw of Marple signed King Charles I's death warrant. During the Chartist Riots in 1842, from the balcony above the door, Mary Ellen Bradshaw-Isherwood clutched her baby son and faced down a mob of Luddites – rioting textile workers who feared new technology would decimate their livelihoods. Benjamin Disraeli referenced this incident in his novel *Sybil,* which explored the plight of England's working classes. Author Christopher Isherwood inherited Marple Hall. His semi-autobiographical work *Goodbye to Berlin* inspired the musical *Cabaret*, but these are not the Hall's most famous connections.

Marple Hall was demolished in 1959, but despite all this history, its true legacy could lie in an unremarkable set of furnishings.

The reason you might think, *Marple sounds familiar* is connected to two sisters who attended an auction of the Hall's contents. Later, one of them wrote in a letter that they had bought some Jacobean oak chairs at the sale.

The sisters were Madge and her younger sibling, Agatha, who was in the process of writing a series of short stories. Once, Madge bet Agatha she couldn't write a 'whodunit' where the reader couldn't guess the killer.

Madge lost the bet spectacularly.

In 1920, her little sis, Agatha Christie, published *The Mysterious Affair at Styles*, which introduced a Belgian detective called Hercule

Poirot. She went on to become the 'Queen of Crime', the world's bestselling novelist, and author of *The Mousetrap*, the world's longest running play.

Miss Marple was another of Christie's famous creations. In a letter to a fan, Christie confirmed that she named her celebrated sleuth after the manor house where she bought the chairs.

Who knew that Greater Manchester was the birthplace of Miss Marple?!

Maybe the character took on some of the poise and timeworn dignity of the town or manor: a quiet, unassuming façade masking intrigue and complexity. And like her namesake, the understated elderly but shrewd detective was not all she seemed.

Our first clue to this came when we crossed the Goyt via a slender and elegantly arched white iron carriage bridge. An owner of the Brabyns estate, Nathaniel Wright, who amassed his fortune from coal mining, commissioned it. Peeping through luxuriant foliage and spanning the sun-kissed river, after two centuries, it still met Wright's criteria – he had wanted a bridge to impress his peers. In 1813, cast iron was a new and untried bridge material. A plaque declared the bridge a listed structure of national importance. It was the North West's first cast iron bridge, and the only one to have survived unaltered and intact.

It was our first hint that pastoral, provincial Marple has more in common with the smokestacks of Stockport than you might imagine.

As we continued through the woods, we caught sight of something monumental hidden among the trees. It reminded me of my first glimpse of the Pont du Gard, a 2,000-year-old Roman aqueduct in France. In all our travels, Pont du Gard remains a highlight and is still one of the best things I've ever seen!

Marple is home to a striking pair of bridges, the Marple Aqueduct, and the Marple Viaduct. They run parallel to each other and stretch across the steep and scenic Goyt Valley. Their golden stones and lofty arches are the telltale evidence that beneath Marple's genteel exterior lies a tale of ambition, industry, and reinvention.

The glittering river, now once again a pastoral haven teeming with wildlife, flowed fast enough to bring the Industrial Revolution to sleepy Marple.

Visionary entrepreneur Samuel Oldknow built the world's largest cotton mill on her banks. He literally refashioned the landscape by diverting the River Goyt – along with the county border it formed between Derbyshire and Cheshire – to create the romantically named Roman Lakes. These became a tourist attraction even in Oldknow's time, although their purpose was purely practical. A series of millponds, waterways, and tunnels, their sole aim was to power the gigantic wheels of Oldknow's industry.

Oldknow was a major sponsor of the Peak Forest Canal. As someone who sought to combine commerce with aesthetics in his grand ambitions, he transferred his canal across the Goyt valley on what is still the UK's tallest masonry-arch aqueduct. He intended the Roman-inspired arches to complement the dramatic scenery. Although constructed between 1794 and 1800, the aqueduct is still in use today and carries the canal 100 feet (30 m) above the river. Marple's flight of 16 locks is among the steepest in Britain, raising boats 210 ft (64 m) in around a mile (1.6 km). Each lock raises the water level around 13 ft (4 m). When I saw it, the access into the first of the Marple Locks reminded me of the entrance to a medieval castle, except that once you'd gone beneath the arch, you faced a lock gate, rather than a portcullis.

The railway bridge, completed much later in 1865, rises even higher than the aqueduct. When viewed from below, the golden arches of the twin bridges seem to interlock and create a scene of enduring majesty amid the serene surroundings of lush woods and waterways.

Yet Oldknow's progressive approach went beyond the bold fusion of form and function. He departed radically from the standard business model of the time. To generate maximum profits for their masters, labourers as young as six or seven were condemned for life to long days of dangerous back-breaking work for poverty wages. Oldknow's utopian ideals sought to improve their lot. He was as prepared to share his success and prosperity with those who helped him rise as he was unafraid to innovate and take risks. In relative terms, he treated his workers well. So well that 3,000 people attended his funeral.

But bold vision comes at a price, and Oldknow ran up enormous debts. Richard Arkwright, whose dad invented the famous Spinning Jenny, bailed him out. When Oldknow died in 1828, Arkwright inherited his estate.

Like much of Marple's heritage, the mill is no longer there. It burned down in 1892, leaving little trace other than the Roman Lakes. Apart from a few eerie ruins dissolving into the woodland, the aqueduct is one of the few remaining testaments to his vision.

Sleepy Marple embraced the roar of the Industrial Revolution only fleetingly, with Samuel Oldknow's grand ventures at its heart. As the mills fell silent, Marple let go of its mechanised ambitions and allowed nature to reclaim its spaces. Marple chose tranquillity over industry and retreated into the serenity of its natural surroundings. Its waterways flowed undisturbed, with echoes of its industrial past lingering only as a faint whisper in the leaves.

By the mid-20th century, Marple had settled back into its gentle, unhurried existence within the margins of the countryside. After its brief flirtation with manufacturing, it contrasted once more with the deteriorating industrialised centres of nearby Stockport and Manchester. It became an attractive refuge, which drew the middle classes who sought calm away from the decay and hustle of the city.

Among those who made the move was the family of a precocious five-year-old, Anthony Howard Wilson.

As an adult, the late great Tony Wilson's life, outlook, and legacy shared surprising parallels with fellow Marple resident, Samuel Oldknow.

Those familiar with bands like Joy Division, New Order, and the Happy Mondays will know him well. Wilson co-founded Factory Records and was the driving force behind the legendary Manchester nightclub The Haçienda.

In the 1990s, Wilson defined an era and emerged as a self-styled cultural trailblazer for the North. He played a pivotal role in reshaping Manchester. He transformed depressed, post-industrial, post-war Manchester into a global hub for music and creativity, and gave her pride and a new identity.

Wilson became so synonymous with his beloved city he was often dubbed 'Mr. Manchester'.

Tony Wilson's wild, chaotic genius always causes a fond smile to play around my lips. When he said, "Choose an arbitrary purpose and stick to it," I understood the meaning of life.

His joyously bonkers philosophies and unorthodox business tactics were heroic but ultimately ruinous. He prioritised vision and societal impact over financial gain. He granted his bands unprecedented artistic freedom and refused to use formal contracts. Artists retained full ownership of their music, while Factory Records had no legal claim to the proceeds from their work. The label basked in creative glory and success – but not profit.

A fine example was New Order's *Blue Monday*.

The bestselling twelve-inch single *of all time* actually cost the company money because its lavish sleeve was so expensive to produce.

And here, I must digress to mention a standout among Factory Records' best concept covers.

The initial 2,000 copies of The Durutti Column's debut album were made of coarse sandpaper, hand-glued by the band themselves. This was an homage to the 1959 book *Mémoires*. In an attempt to defy the norms that defined fine art and collectable objects, its sandpaper dust jacket damaged books shelved next to it, any surface where it was placed, and even abraded the reader!

Any money made by New Order and Factory Records was diverted mostly into propping up The Haçienda nightclub. Despite its iconic status, the club struggled financially from the outset. New Order's bassist, Peter Hook, claimed Wilson founded The Haçienda not for profit, but to provide a hangout for punks like him who had nowhere to go.

The Factory team had zero experience in designing and building a club. They viewed this as a positive, since it freed them from preconceptions. In 1981, this deficiency resulted in a minor budget overrun for the build.

From £70,000 to £344,000 – which equates to over £3-million in today's terms.

But the iconic interior by award-winning designer, Ben Kelly, was amazing!

Once it opened, the club failed to claw back its debts. In fact, it seldom broke even. Its primary source of income was alcohol sales, but its acid house and rave culture clientele preferred drugs such as ecstasy, which they thoughtfully provided themselves.

The drug scene attracted gang violence. This not only forced a huge additional expenditure on security, but incited a protracted battle with the police and other authorities keen to revoke the club's licence.

Contributions from other random incidents that are the stuff of legend help sum up the whole delightfully shambolic Factory/Haçienda story. My favourite tale recounts how, one New Year's Eve, indoor fireworks set the club's entire takings on fire.

The Haçienda pioneered house music and hosted a stellar cast of imported and homegrown talent. From global icon Madonna's first UK performance to a musical Who's Who of the '90s: The Smiths, Oasis, and The Stone Roses, in addition to bands from the Factory Records stable.

Even so, in June 1997, after a decade and a half at the beating heart of 'Madchester', The Haçienda lost its licence and its doors closed for good.

Five years later, a residential developer bulldozed the former yacht builder's warehouse and erased its physical legacy.

Though separated by centuries, Oldknow and Wilson exemplify the spirit of visionaries driven by bold ideas, defiance of convention, and a desire to reshape their worlds. Both were set on creating something transformative. Oldknow in the realm of industrial innovation and community building. Wilson fostering a cultural revolution. Creative energy and financial strain punctuated both of their lives, and each left a legacy of ambition that prioritised vision over economic stability, which underscores Wilson's famous quote:

"You either make money, or you make history."

He had a point.

I can't think of any legendary accountants.

Wilson's crazy, accidental, purposeful, rebellious, terrifying, thrilling, hedonistic, unapologetic, groundbreaking, and impractical achievements were the embodiment of this. In conventional terms of profit and loss, his endeavours were disastrous, but success depends on your view, and what you set out to achieve.

As an experimental piece of conceptual art, the Factory/Haçienda fantasy was flawless.

Too often, society defines success by the narrow, one-dimensional criterion of money. An approach which completely misses out everything that matters. Like happiness, fulfilment, kindness, change, passion, and love.

If you innovate, you must accept failure or unexpected consequences. Perfection lies in imperfection, because at least it's not mundane.

All of which resonates with a pair of mavericks who had slipped the shackles of convention in their wildly impractical Manky Monstrosity, on a trip that had become so much more Manchester than Mongolia.

Chapter 21

More Manchester Than Mongolia

"**D**ress like you are meeting the in-laws for the first time," was one piece of advice we had garnered on securing a favourable outcome from our visa appointment.

"Bring everything in quadruplicate; originals mean originals; and if in doubt, bring any extra documents to prove your address, income, or anything else."

We had done all that, but when you own only 10 kg of clothing each, the dress code proved problematic. When dealing with a bureaucratic institution, the person behind the desk holds all the power. We knew we would be at their mercy – and we were applying to Italy. The most stylish nation on earth. Could they reject us for being fashion philistines?

Determined to make a positive first impression and in view of the ongoing heatwave, we donned our cleanest, least crumpled T-shirts and shorts, and strapped on our smartest, or should I say only, pairs of sandals.

In the end, with four dogs in tow, we'd decided to bite the bullet. At 7 a.m., well before rush hour, we parked The Beast on a large piece of waste ground in central Manchester, near Ardwick Station. We could have got there by train from Marple. However, since one of us had to look after the pups while the other went in to the visa application centre, we opted to do it with all home comforts and as much tea as necessary on tap.

Such is the advantage of having your home on wheels.

Trains rattled over the blackened red brick viaducts as I waited a couple of hours for Mark to come back. The car park gradually filled up, although the chap who'd charged a mere £10 for the day kindly made sure he positioned us for an easy exit.

When I entered the sterile white interior of the faceless office block, it exuded an atmosphere of quiet bustle with an undertone of muffled desperation. I followed the signs for Italian visas, passing rooms full of people lodging visa applications for all over the world. I sensed many had much more than a ski season in Italy riding on a successful application.

I handed over the certified copies of bank accounts in triplicate, along with the originals of my birth certificate, marriage certificate, and passport.

I hadn't realised I'd be surrendering the entire master file of my identity!

As the youngster across the desk from me bundled them up with an elastic band and plopped them in an envelope, I felt profoundly uncomfortable.

If they lost them, would I cease to exist?

How long would they keep them?

On the off chance that the international borders did open for an indeterminate period while they processed our application, having no papers would preclude us from travelling abroad.

Although venturing anywhere, even in Britain, suddenly became uncertain.

***

Mark was in demand.

The DVSA (Driver and Vehicle Standards Agency) called him up! It seems that after telling all the ruddy foreigners who were in Britain nicking all our jobs to go home, Brexit might have caused a teensy deficit of truck drivers.

This plunged the UK into a fuel shortage. Brexit had already disrupted fuel supplies, but without truckers, there was no one to deliver the little fuel there was.

Then all the grannies who do two miles per week started to panic buy, thinking they might be denied the chance to head out for a slow drive on a Sunday afternoon to hold up all the traffic.

Besides the dearth of fuel, further problems were forecast. The scarcity of drivers and immigrant seasonal workers also sparked fears of food shortages. I'd read a headline stating that the surge in natural gas and power prices to record levels had already caused some small energy suppliers to collapse, with more predicted to follow. Should the UK experience severe winter weather, speculation was rife concerning potential power blackouts. Spiralling costs for energy and transportation, plus labour shortages, led to warnings of rising inflation.

I had to shout, "Hurrah for Brexit! Brexiteers wanted to go back to 'the good old days' and here we are back in the 1970s, with rampant inflation and power cuts!"

For his part, Mark gave due consideration to the government's request for him to return to work as a lorry driver because 'Your Country Needs You!'

He took at least a millisecond to arrive at a decision.

Absolutely no chance!

The Prime Minister, Boris Johnson, addressed the nation with reassurances that the fuel situation was under control. However, The Johnson and factual accuracy were never comfortable bedfellows, and the Petrol Retailers Association simultaneously reported that three-quarters of petrol stations had run out of fuel.

Determined to make light of the situation, Mark issued an edict. "I think the Petrol Retailers Association should rename themselves the Association of Rumpy Pumpies."

I smiled and replied, "It's a good job we've got 700 miles of diesel on board. If we tried to fill up The Beast, I reckon we might get lynched..."

We had a long, hot journey back to Foxton Locks, where we planned to stay ahead of our pre-MOT service and checkup at Crouch's.

All the way there, I had been promising myself a beer.

At 6 p.m., we walked down the locks, deciding which of the two pubs to choose. We decided on Bridge 61, where a few canal boaters holding golden pints sat at the outside tables.

"You won't get a beer here," they told us.

"Why not?" we asked.

"Because it's closed."

"What?"

"Because it's winter!"

It was still 86°F (30°C), and we were in our shorts!

"The Bell at Gumley is open, and it's pie night on Tuesday!"

As if we needed any more encouragement to walk across the field to the village in the September sunshine. It was warm enough to dine al fresco in the balmy evening air. The pie, the beer, and the welcome were stellar.

Wednesday was steak night at The Bell, but after a day spent hiding from the heat, we strolled along the shady canal towpath to the Black Horse in Foxton.

But bad news awaited.

We received a phone call from the MOT centre to say they'd cancelled our appointment because of COVID.

We phoned everyone, but no one could offer another lorry test at such short notice.

This was disastrous!

No MOT would render our home not road legal.

Although with a broken screen wash bottle, our chances of passing already seemed remote.

***

Twice in my life, I have professed to a stranger that I wanted to have their babies.

I made the first proposal to a surprised-looking Italian on a campsite on the shores of Lake Garda. He volunteered to repair the front of our caravan when he noticed it propped up on a giant tin of apricot halves because the jockey wheel had broken.

He looked bemused and said, "Just a coffee is fine!"

The second happened when we arrived back at Crouch's early the following morning.

Chris, the engineer, removed a wasps' nest from our pollen filters and a bird's nest from the rear of our front bumper. He serviced The Beast and let us loose with his jet washer, so that we could "present her nicely" for her non-existent roadworthiness test.

But most important to the success of our sadly out-of-reach MOT, Crouch's had found and fitted a new windscreen wash bottle!

Matter-of-factly, with not so much as a flourish, they installed a part for which I'd scoured the internet for the last three months. They didn't even mention it. Squeaking and jumping up and down with my hands over my mouth, I just noticed it!

But with a cancelled appointment, our victory was hollow...

Until we shared our MOT misery with Head Honcho, Dave.

He said, "Give our test centre a bell. We always have something that needs doing, so we keep a few dates up our sleeve."

At that point, I think Mark might have wanted to have his babies too!

Chapter 22

"You Have A Pig's Nose!" Adventure Overland Show

"Ah. You heff a pig's nose!" the man declared. His Dutch accent added a musical lilt to his words.

"Thank you. That's the nicest thing anyone has said to me today!" I replied.

He tilted his head, unsure whether I was serious, and pointed at a small cylindrical protrusion on the right side of The Beast's bonnet.

"*Eine Schweinenase*," he explained. "All NATO army trucks heff them. For jump-starting in the field. It connects directly to the battery."

Later, I stifled a giggle as I shared the interaction and my newfound knowledge with Mark. Living with The Beast was like unwrapping a never-ending gift: another day, another peculiarity of our truck revealed.

We were at the Adventure Overland Show in Stratford-upon-Avon, where the social media group LorryLife Campers UK had invited us to display The Beast on their stand.

As well as an opportunity to meet like-minded people, they offered free entry into the show and free camping at the racecourse, a short walk along the river from the medieval town centre. It hadn't taken long to decide!

The Adventure Overland Show is the UK's largest get-together of camper conversions, off-road, and overland vehicles. Although a few of the folks we'd met online would be there, for Mark and me, it was the first time we'd physically encountered anyone who lived and adventured in a truck. Since lockdowns had curtailed so many overlanders' travel plans, the show had an exceptional turnout.

In the UK, four-wheel-drive, cab-over-engine MAN and DAF lorries are popular base vehicles for overland conversions. Designed for military use, they are robust, reliable, and have a wide support network in Europe and beyond. Plus, having the cab above the engine makes the truck shorter and more manoeuvrable. Unlike our Volvo, the British armed forces used them, so they often pop up at military surplus sales for reasonable prices.

At the show, amid a sea of four-wheeled DAFs, MANs, and Mercedes-Benz Unimogs, our enormous six-wheeled Belgian Beast, with her prominent bull-nose, attracted men like moths to a lantern's bewitching flame.

Mark spent the first morning under The Beast with John, greasing his nipples.

Beneath the truck, John disclosed to Mark that his previous greasing hadn't done much good. John advised, "If you use the vehicle daily, you should grease the prop shaft weekly. Say, if your gearbox fails, you can feather it and still get somewhere. But if your prop shaft fails, it's curtains."

So far, received advice on greasing intervals stretched from six-monthly to weekly, depending on who you spoke to. Perhaps it was just something we needed to monitor.

Naturally, on entering historic Stratford, birthplace of The Bard himself, William Shakespeare, our first stop was PC World. This was because Mark's new laptop was still playing up. As we would be in one place for a week, we figured it might give them sufficient time to mend it.

"If we have to send it away twice and it's not fixed," they said, "you can have a new laptop." Since PC World in Bournemouth had already sent it off for repair, we hoped, quietly, it was unfixable and would be replaced with something more reliable.

In other tech news, my watch had stopped working on the 13th, which seemed rather portentous. However, the Timpson's in the retail park had me up and running with a replacement battery in fewer than two minutes.

Our laundry bid was less successful. When I took a bag of smalls into the launderette next to the supermarket, I was surprised to find myself in an Aladdin's cave of enchantment, festooned with smoked sausages and ripe with the aroma of exotic cheeses. A dark-haired gentleman smiled and told me, "We're a Polish delicatessen. Until a week ago, we were a launderette, but we haven't got around to switching the sign."

Because we were taking full advantage of discounted city centre camping before and after the free nights at the show, we were the first of the LorryLife Campers UK crowd to arrive. Paul, the group's founder, was working, so he was not due until later in the week. As such, he had put out a call for a volunteer to manage parking. Ever unable to keep my head below the parapet, I had responded, "I'll do it if no one else will."

Of course, no one else would, which resulted in a headache for me – and a stand whose layout changed with each additional guest. Most plonked themselves wherever they wanted. Paul told me there was a video of the previous year's setup, but I couldn't find it. So, when a self-proclaimed veteran of the show arrived, I was happy to delegate to him. However, his eager encouragement for new arrivals to, "Just park anywhere," left me and Mark herding trucks as though they were a wayward flock of ants. We tried to persuade everyone to park around the outside to leave a space in the centre because Paul had said he was expecting a large truck, although we weren't completely certain that the large truck was not our Beast...

Finally, Paul arrived in his grey 7.5-tonne DAF T244, Milly.

We ran over to shake Paul's hand. "It's great to meet you at last!" I said, and enthusiastically relinquished my parking responsibilities.

With Roxy, his tiny rescue Jack Russell terrier, tucked under his arm, Paul explained a bit about Milly and his lifestyle.

"I bought Milly after my divorce," he told us. "Paying for a house *and* child maintenance was completely unaffordable. I'd considered a motorhome, but I got the idea of a truck from visiting this show. The big trucks blew me away. They offer so much more room for a family."

7.5 tonnes is a magic number for drivers of a certain age. Anyone who passed their UK car (Category B) driving test before 1st January 1997 has 'grandfather rights' – an automatic entitlement to drive 3.5 to 7.5-tonne (Category C1) vehicles, such as Paul's.

"Milly's chassis came from a military charity," he continued. "To keep the weight under 7.5 tonnes, I found a company to fit a composite plastic body, like a refrigerated lorry, and all aluminium roof racks and fittings. Sometimes, I put an inflatable sofa on the roof rack above the cab. It's a great place to chill when you're parked in the countryside, and it gives a fantastic vantage at festivals. My kids love it!

"I wanted to escape the system. Now I'm in the truck full-time, I'm better off than I've ever been. I work three days a week. My company lets me park outside overnight, and then I spend the other four days travelling. I love the freedom and the community."

As more people arrived, the variety of 'built not bought' vehicles amazed us. Since The Adventure Overland Show incorporated the International Campervan Show, we were getting two shows in one, with a vast and quirky array of vehicles. The quiet time before the exhibition opened to the public yielded plenty of opportunities to look around and chat with the owners. There were over a hundred custom campervan conversions, a large gathering of modified Land Rovers, a few dozen trucks, ambulances, and fire engines, plus a small selection of serious military vehicles. The biggest of these was an ex-German MAN KAT1 8×8 high mobility carrier, with canvas sides to the front and a hard rear section, which the owner had converted into a camper. I longed to discover the extraordinary stories behind them all, but there were so many. It was impossible to see everything!

Even on the LorryLife Campers UK stand, we had an eclectic range of campers. It truly was a field of dreams.

The 'large' truck we had awaited might have been the rather impressive 'Queenie'. We stopped to chat with her creator, Si.

"It was Mum and Dad's dream to travel once they retired," he said, "but sadly, Dad passed away before that could happen. I built Queenie so my mum, Carol, could still get out and see the world."

Si traced his hands over the silvery-grey weathered planks that formed Queenie's body. "The accommodation is basically a 1930s cattle transport railway car. I bought the frame for scrap because it was completely burned out. I rebuilt it and mounted it onto the back of this 18-tonne DAF truck. The box lifts off, so if we ever fancy a change, she could become a houseboat!"

A chimney from Queenie's wood-burning stove protruded from her roof. It was directly in front of a raised half-storey to her rear, which housed Si's mezzanine bed. "She sleeps four," Si said as he gave us the full tour. Light from the sliding patio doors on her side, and reclaimed vintage stained glass panels flooded the inside. I loved her tactile live-edge worktops, but the best thing for me was her bathtub, made from half an old whiskey barrel!

A long soak in a hot bath with a book is the only comfort I miss from our conventional life.

At the front of the LorryLife stand, a 1980 American school bus the colour of an organic egg yolk demanded everyone's attention. 'Skoolies' make light and spacious residences, but with so many windows, are difficult to insulate fully, and prone to condensation. 'Queen Bee' was 36 ft (11 m) long. Her owners, Allison and Simon, welcomed us into a space that was as sunny and bright as the day. Like our Beast, Queen Bee was a lockdown conversion, but executed on a remarkably small budget.

"We rescued her from having her backside chopped off by a hobbyist to make a car transporter!" they said. "We couldn't get materials, so we used pallet wood to line the walls. The rest is stuff we already owned, bought on Marketplace, or bartered. I swapped a chair I had for a larger water tank!"

As we entered, Simon pointed out a white-painted set of drawers with a natural wooden top. "That came from our house. We cut off the legs and fitted it over the wheel arch. The drawers aren't on runners, so they don't fly open when we're driving."

He indicated the luxurious chocolate-coloured velour couch, complemented by a selection of scatter cushions in shades of pale primrose and buttercup yellow.

"We got that sofa bed for £40," Simon said, before leading us to the kitchen area, further back in the bus.

"We bought the wooden worktop from a chap on Marketplace who had two offcuts left over. A conversion doesn't need full lengths, so it was ample for our needs."

Of course, a conversion is never truly finished, though.

Simon added, "We've already removed a table we didn't use and replaced it with more worktop."

The centrepiece was surely the curvaceous, oversized Smeg American-style refrigerator. Its bold and joyful sunflower hue tied everything together, turning Queen Bee into a real showstopper.

"You didn't get that on Marketplace, did you?" I asked.

"I did. It cost £100 because of slight damage on the interior freezer door!"

"She's sensational!" I said to Simon. "What are your plans?"

"We still have our house, but we're in the process of downsizing into the bus. She's our retirement plan!"

Back at The Beast, our view from bed was a pleasing line of blunt noses – a smart lineup of DAF trucks, whose rugged outlines glinted in the sunlight. For the first time in years, we felt completely at home – not only in our truck, but in the company of people who understood why we lived this way.

Our neighbours, Charlotte and Stuart, The Orkney Overlanders, introduced themselves and showed us around Dinky, their grey self-built DAF.

Dinky is one of my favourite conversions. Inside, she is like a cosy Swiss chalet, with wooden tongue-and-groove walls and a homely log burner. She was a post-lockdown truck, but even without the pandemic, a lack of materials on remote islands such as Orkney is a fact of life. With COVID travel restrictions in place throughout 2020, they couldn't leave the island to source any goods. As such, Stuart built everything himself from scratch, including the habitation box.

"We fabricated the frame from steel angle. Once we'd welded it together, my brother lifted the front, and I reversed the DAF beneath it. Then, we pushed it up onto the bed of the truck, and covered it in 1 mm galvanised steel."

Charlotte explained how they had repurposed the sofa cushions from an old caravan. "We made the tabletop from a piece of the truck's original wooden floor. The windows are completely homemade: steel frames double-glazed with left-over COVID screens."

"Dinky gives us flexibility to travel for work – we help others with their builds through the summer, then in winter, we escape to somewhere warmer with whatever we've earned or saved."

When they came to look inside The Beast, it was whiskey o'clock. Mark revealed he'd broken a spanner and the tinny, tiny torque wrench we'd had for the caravan checking The Beast's wheel nuts. Stuart shared the benefit of his engineering experience.

"When you have a bigger truck, you need bigger stuff!"

Over a few drams of our favourite Scotch, we cemented a lasting friendship.

I attended several of the talks given by seasoned overlanders, jotting down tips and priceless nuggets of advice – never suspecting how soon I'd need to put some of their guidance into practice...

"What's the first thing you should do in an emergency?" one speaker asked the audience. "That's right. You make a cup of tea!" He answered his own rhetorical question. "It gives you a moment to think clearly and get a grip before you tackle the problem."

He also shared that, "Parking with the vehicle bonnet up is the international distress signal."

Then, he recounted how, "If you're stopped by dodgy police officers in dodgy places, it's always good to make a show of taking down their badge number. That way, you'll soon find out if their intent is true, or they're demanding a bribe, but *don't* try to photograph them... Carry a few bottles of cheap whiskey, and only *ever* hand over photocopies of documents."

I drank in their wisdom and intrepid tales. Spellbound, I listened to wild, dust-choked tales of adventures in far-flung corners of the earth, told by people who hadn't just daydreamed about visiting Mongolia – they had driven there.

The weekend passed in a blur of visitors, Bingo questions, dog walks, and hurried detours to view the trade stands. One seller had a smoke-bubble generator – an irresistible lure for Rosie. As she did once in the market square in Wrocław, Poland, she wowed the crowd by leaping with athletic precision to burst the drifting spheres, although this time, each snap generated a tiny puff of smoke.

For anyone dreaming of van life or lorry life, events like this are an essential pilgrimage. Wandering between the vehicles, hearing their owners' stories, and soaking up the creativity and ingenuity on display is not only inspiring. It's a reminder that these vehicles aren't mere machines; they're passports to freedom, born of passion, grit, and a satisfying streak of rebellion.

As a couple who had once hauled a caravan over the Carpathian Mountains, we'd always felt like misfits in the caravanning community. But as campfires cast a flickering glow across the gathering, and the scent of wood smoke curled its way into the star-studded night, laughter mingled with the drifting sparks. We knew we'd found our tribe.

Here, we were among unconventional kindred spirits. Restless souls united by the belief that home isn't a place on a map.

It's wherever the journey takes you.

Chapter 23

Sent to Coventry & The English Game of Thrones

A s we left the Overland Show, we had a really rubbish afternoon. I blamed the government.

It started with the ongoing saga of trying to get our Italian visas so that post Brexit, we could continue with our seasonal ski trips. Yet now, even getting the visa required additional bureaucracy. It turned out we needed a criminal records check, which would take two weeks and cost an extra £55 each on top of the huge fee we'd already paid.

Then, when we went to buy lunch supplies at the supermarket, they only had Cheddar and stale bread. We love British cheese, but our sandwich table has become accustomed to the tongue-tingling variety added to it by French Brie, Italian Pecorino, or Swiss Emmental. But post Brexit, such exotic foreign delights were not available. And with a lack of seasonal workers due to Brexit-imposed immigration changes, we hadn't seen a Savoy cabbage since the fateful day that Britain parted company from the EU.

Import problems forced us to buy emergency supermarket dog food, because we couldn't find The Fab Four's favourite brands anywhere on the internet.

There were also the aforementioned fuel shortages, whose existence the glorious Johnson denied.

We had planned to drive to another Self Build Get Together at Wantage but were wary of squandering diesel on a 200-mile round trip, because we would have to return to Tamworth for the emergency MOT granted by Crouch. If we pulled into a service station with The Beast, we were conscious that we might trigger a small uprising. We didn't want a mob to run us off the forecourt, pelting us with jerrycans.

As we arrived at our park-up for the night near Kenilworth – billed as 'a quiet and peaceful spot right on the Greensand Way' – we saw it had vanished under a vast desert of earthworks. This was HS2 – the ill-fated 'High Speed 2' rail link that was supposed to connect London and Birmingham with the northern cities of Manchester and Leeds. Instead, in great British tradition, it was running years late, and colossally over budget.

Time was getting on, so we sent ourselves to Coventry.

We plumped to park at a pub, and went in for dinner, only to be told,

"We can't serve you any food because we can't hire a chef, and there is no beer because of the transport problems. There's a fish and chip shop down the road. You're welcome to grab a takeaway and eat it in here."

On the plus side, since Brexit had devastated the export market, there was plenty of fish. Prior to Britain's bid to rid itself of its horrible neighbour, Europe purchased almost half of the UK fishing fleet's total catch.

Good old Tory policies.

Mark and I would go and protest, but under the broad sweep of the proposed Police, Crime, Sentencing and Courts Bill, we would probably be arrested, and that would scupper our attempts to get a criminal records check for our Italian visa!

***

We repaired to Bosworth, where on 22nd August, 1485, the Yorkist King, Richard III, had a much worse afternoon than us. On that date, he became the last King of England to lose his life in battle.

The Battle of Bosworth Field crackles like a fault line through English history. It was a decisive blow, which concluded a family feud that got out of hand – namely the Wars of the Roses. This was a decades-long civil war between the houses of Lancaster and York over the English throne.

Bosworth ended the Plantagenet royal dynasty, which had ruled England for 300 years. They did some good stuff. The first of them, Henry II, laid the foundations for English governance and the legal system, giving us common law and trial by jury.

Unfortunately, Henry's youngest son, Bad King John (the clue is in the name), undid many of his father's achievements. He only became king because his older brothers, Henry and Richard the Lionheart, died. He secured his succession when he imprisoned – and possibly murdered – his remaining elder sibling, Geoffrey.

His reign was a disaster. He lost Normandy, bled the country dry with heavy taxation, and ruled with arbitrary cruelty. Eventually, an angry group of barons turned on him and forced him to sign the

Magna Carta.

This document, drawn up in 1215, was essentially a medieval bill of rights.

Over 800 years later, its key principle still resonates. It declared that no one – not even the king – was above the law.

Which underscores the point that in today's troubled times, where voters deem convicted felons and inveterate liars fit to lead the world's principal democracies, a lesson we can take from history is that nobody ever learns lessons from history.

However, a small rebel army from France actually *made* history on 22nd August, 1485, when they seized the day.

We set off on the Battle of Bosworth Trail to discover how England's very own Game of Thrones reached its brutal finale.

Chapter 24

Bosworth: Backstabbing, Betrayal, & A Body in a Car Park

C ontemporary sources noted two ill-matched armies, separated by a marsh, near the town of Market Bosworth.

Yorkist King Richard III's superior force of 10,000 faced Henry Tudor's 5,000 men. A mysterious third army, numbering around 6,000, stood between the two main forces, under the command of Lord Thomas Stanley.

Henry Tudor was an exiled Lancastrian with a distant claim to the English throne. That said, King Richard's claim was also questionable.

In April 1483, Richard's older brother, King Edward IV, died unexpectedly, aged only 40. Before his death, he appointed Richard as Lord Protector to his two male heirs until the eldest, 12-year-old Prince Edward, was mature enough to rule as King Edward V.

A month after Edward IV's death, in May 1483, Richard lodged his nephews in the royal residence inside the Tower of London. This was ostensibly for their protection while preparations for Edward's coronation went ahead, although Richard delayed the ceremony repeatedly.

The following month, Richard declared his nephews illegitimate and seized the throne for himself.

By late June 1483, only two months after the King's death, both boys had vanished – presumed murdered. No conclusive evidence has ever revealed who was responsible, and for centuries, the fate of the 'Princes in the Tower' remains one of England's most enduring historical mysteries, frequently with Richard in the frame of suspicion.

Also lacking definitive proof was Richard's (and Edward's) involvement in orchestrating the execution of his only other surviving Plantagenet brother, George, Duke of Clarence, in 1478. George was older than Richard, and therefore a rival for the throne. Accused of treason for attempting to undermine King Edward, legend has it that George met his death by drowning in a butt of malmsey wine.

Back at Bosworth, the third protagonist was a notorious master of strategic ambiguity and vague allegiance. Lord Thomas Stanley had successfully navigated a treacherous path through decades of dynastic bloodshed by pledging just enough loyalty to the houses of both York and Lancaster to stay in favour, no matter who had the upper hand in the War of the Roses. His preference for vacillation over valour made him an enduring survivor in an age where any bold declarations of fealty could prove fatal if the other side was suddenly in the ascendancy.

Thomas Stanley was King Richard's Steward of the Royal Household, which surely rendered him loyal to his king.

Except that Stanley's wife, Margaret Beaufort, was Henry Tudor's mum.

This made the chap trying to grab Richard's crown Stanley's stepson, which presented Stanley with both a huge dilemma – and potentially a lot to gain.

Prior to the clash, Stanley refused to commit to either side.

Slippery Stanley was renowned for arriving late for battles. Often, he missed them completely!

When Henry Tudor first came ashore in Wales, Richard ordered Thomas and his younger brother, Sir William Stanley, to attack the usurper. Thomas said he couldn't, claiming he had the 'sweating sickness' – a malady better known today as 'man flu'.

Richard III was wise to Stanley's conflict of interest and took precautions. To ensure his loyalty in battle, Richard took George, Lord Strange, Stanley's son and heir, hostage. If Stanley failed to support his king, Richard vowed he would kill George on the battlefield.

On the eve of battle, Richard sent a messenger to remind Stanley of this arrangement.

Stanley's alleged reply, "Sire, I have other sons..." may not be entirely factual, but illustrates this man's cold-hearted ruthlessness.

On the morning of 22nd August, the Duke of Norfolk lined up on Richard's right flank. Heavy gunfire from King Richard's forces may have forced the Earl of Oxford to lead the bulk of Henry Tudor's troops around the marsh to attack Norfolk, using a classic wedge formation. Oxford defeated Norfolk's army on behalf of Henry Tudor and killed the Duke.

The *Song of Lady Bessye*, written in the early 16th century for the Stanley family, states Norfolk fell near a windmill. High-status archaeological finds clustered in an area called Mill Field, where the old Dadlington windmill once stood, could well pinpoint the position of the Duke's last stand.

Meanwhile, on Richard's left flank, the Earl of Northumberland did not move: perhaps hemmed in by the marsh in front and the Stanleys to his side. As Henry advanced, Richard saw his opportunity and gambled everything. In a gallant show of courage, Richard charged across the battlefield with a cohort of mounted knights to kill Henry and end the battle decisively.

It was a brilliant ruse, and Richard apparently got within a sword's length of Henry. Richard would likely have emerged victorious, were it not for one single, treacherous decision.

Stanley's third army joined the fray and launched their attack.

Against Richard.

Finally, the Stanleys had chosen their side.

When his horse got bogged down in the mire, sources report Richard fought valiantly on foot. "In the thickest press of his foes," Richard III vowed to win or die as King of England, but Richard's supposed allies had turned on him at the decisive moment. They cut him off from his army and hacked him down. Sources report a blow to the head with a halberd killed him.

The Stanleys removed Richard's crown, then slung his naked, mutilated body across a horse's back and took him to Leicester. There, they displayed the body in public to prove the king was dead. Afterwards, the Grey Friars reportedly gave Richard a hasty burial in their church.

In nearby Stoke Golding, at Garbrodys Hill, renamed around 1485 and still known today as Crown Hill, Stanley unofficially crowned his stepson King of England.

And so, the Tudor dynasty began.

History is written by the victors, so a century later, Shakespeare certainly got a worthy villain to work with – an evil hunchbacked murderer with a withered arm.

As for Richard, his whereabouts remained unknown for over 500 years.

Then in 2012, archaeological detective work, combined with plucky citizen science, culminated in one of Britain's most remarkable archaeological finds.

Remarkable for reasons that far surpassed its profound historical importance.

Philippa Langley, a screenwriter and dedicated member of the Richard III Society, had long suspected that Richard III's much-maligned reputation stemmed from Tudor propaganda. She also believed his final resting place was not lost – merely overlooked.

Acting on historical documents, Langley identified a likely burial site. In the 1500s, during the dissolution of the monasteries, Tudor's son, Henry VIII, demolished Leicester's former Greyfriars Church. However, it lived on in the street names Grey Friars and Friar Lane. In the 21st century, it had long been tarmacked over to become a council car park.

When she visited the site, Philippa felt a strong sense – almost a gut instinct – that she was standing on the right spot.

Then, things got wonderfully surreal.

Philippa noticed a large white letter 'R' painted on one of the parking bays. It merely meant the space was 'Reserved' – obviously nothing to do with 'Richard'. Yet standing over the 'R' triggered a peculiar emotional response in her. Enough for her to persuade the archaeologists to start their excavation there.

On the very first day of the dig, directly beneath the 'R', archaeologists unearthed an astonishingly well-preserved human skeleton.

Designated simply 'Skeleton 1,' the remains showed signs of battle trauma, including fatal blows to the skull and injuries consistent with an attack launched against someone unmounted. There were also wounds inflicted after death, perhaps as humiliation.

The spine had a severe curvature, indicative of scoliosis, which supported some descriptions of Richard's hunched back.

Historically, the location of Skeleton 1 would have lain within the choir of the old Greyfriars Church.

Impressive evidence for sure, but purely circumstantial.

It needed further corroboration.

In time, radiocarbon dating placed the bones firmly in the time-frame of Richard III's death. Then, scientists compared DNA isolated from the skeleton to genetic material from known living descendants of Richard III's sister.

The match was conclusive.

In early 2013, officials confirmed that Skeleton 1, the body in the car park, was indeed Richard III.

***

Usually, I get a deep sense of connection to the past from visiting such sites, but as we walked through rolling hills along marked trails around the battlefield, I said to Mark,

"I don't feel anything here."

A look inside the Bosworth Battlefield Heritage Centre soon revealed why.

After the Princes in the Tower and the body of a king, there was a third mystery disappearance.

Ambion Hill is a prominent feature in the Leicestershire landscape. Scholars identified it as the battle site. After all, it looked the part – and folklore said it was. For centuries, visitors flocked there, drawn by tales of Richard III's last stand, sipping the waters from King Richard's Well, and visiting a solemn limestone cairn erected to mark the spot where the king had heroically met his demise.

Leicestershire County Council even built an award-winning visitor centre there in 1974. Complete with exhibits, historical reconstructions, and what we can now politely call "imaginative" signage, which outlined the unfolding story of the conflict that altered the course of English history.

The only snag?

They built it in the wrong place!

Between 2005 and 2009, archaeologists using historical mapping and advanced metal detecting technology found a range of 15th-century weaponry and artefacts in farmer Alf Oliver's wheat field two miles away. It straddled Fen Lane, a former Roman road. The largest cannonball turned up behind Alf's barn. They nicknamed it 'The Holy Grapefruit'. However, the most crucial find was a gilded solid silver boar, Richard's personal emblem, found in a place called Fen Hole.

Richard dished out a lot of boar insignias to his followers, but for mass distribution, he made them from base materials like lead or pewter. A piece crafted from a precious metal suggests it belonged to a close member of his retinue. The only other one like it resides in the British Museum.

The names Fen Lane and Fen Hole also yield a very important clue.

If you remember, a marshy area played a critical role in Henry Tudor's victory.

Tudor used the soft ground to protect the flank of his much smaller force. Infamously, Richard lost his horse in a mire and was cut down – pledging his kingdom for a horse, according to Shakespeare.

We watched the sunset from the top of Ambion Hill. Flags on the summit cracked and snapped in the wind, echoing the musket fire of long-dead armies whose insignia they bore. They flung their legacy into the soft peachy twilight.

The consequences of that muddy skirmish rippled far beyond the homely English landscape that stretched out before us. The Battle of Bosworth was not merely the bloody finale of a dynastic feud; it marked a fundamental shift in England's political, cultural, and social trajectory. More than just the fall of Richard III and the end of the 300-year Plantagenet rule, it sounded the death knell for medieval England.

The Tudors rose from the wreckage and ushered in a new era of strong centralised monarchy. They sowed the seeds of the English Renaissance, religious transformation through the Reformation, and the first steps towards a modern British state. From the ashes of betrayal, battlefield cunning, and backroom bartering emerged a dynasty that would shape British – and world – events for generations.

History took a sharp turn that day, and its impact continues to define the very fabric of the country.

Standing in the quiet Leicestershire countryside, where cannon once thundered and betrayal decided a crown, I found it hard to imagine the seismic legacy left behind. Yet that is the strange magic of history – how a single event can shape centuries.

Richard may have lost everything that day: his throne, his life, his reputation, and for a time even his grave – but his story remains deeply woven into the national narrative and his ghost still looms large.

As we would discover ourselves in the near future: sometimes, all it takes is a moment in the mud to change the course of everything.

Chapter 25

The Curse of Ironbridge, Shropshire

We'd been touring the UK for three-and-a-half months since we finished converting our beloved 24.5 tonne Belgian Army lorry. To our delight, she passed her MOT. Following frenetic quests for elusive parts, it seemed the universe had decided to cut us a tiny, hard-won break.

But after Ironbridge, it all went wrong.

Ironbridge was a blast in more ways than one. Our park-up at the remains of the Bedlam Furnaces was only a few hundred yards from the historic iron bridge in the centre, from which the town takes its name.

A small terraced garden above the furnace ruins was perfect for a doggie stretch on the evening we arrived. At the top of the hill, just beyond the gardens, we discovered The Golden Ball pub. They gave us such a welcome, it became our local for the duration of our stay.

A voice greeted us the second we walked in.

"Hiya – I met you at Sainsbury's in Telford!"

It was Matt, a chap who came to ask about The Beast while we were doing our shopping.

"I live round the corner from here!"

Talk about coincidence. He called over his wife, Helen, and her friend Karen to say, "Hi"."

Within moments, a crowd of children had flocked around our four cute furball pooches. The barmaid smiled and took our order for their special offer, pizza and a pint for £10, while we knelt on the floor to supervise the kiddie-puppy love session. When we finally sat down properly, we struck up a conversation with Connie and Tom at the next table. They knew Matt, Helen, and Karen, and when they found out why we were in Ironbridge, they invited us all to sit with them.

"You're living our dream lifestyle!" they said.

Tom was from Germany; a proud nation of overland truck lovers. One of the world's ultimate overland and 4x4 shows is the *Abenteuer & Allrad* which takes place in Bad Kissingen, Bavaria, every June.

Four pints of foamin' ale later, we were still protesting that we don't really drink. We properly sealed our bibulous claim to temperance when Tom and Connie came back to see The Beast and we opened a bottle of whiskey for a nightcap – or two. And some wine for the girls.

Connie and Tom returned the following lunchtime to join in the van life fun.

Jaqui next door took a photo of The Beast with her smaller neighbours, as we were all parked neatly in descending size,

"It reminds me of the old *Frost Report 'Class'* sketch, with John Cleese, Ronnie Barker, and Ronnie Corbett" she said. "'I look down on him, because I am upper class...'"

A lovely vintage VW (Volkswagen) camper pulled onto the gravel.

By now, the car park was full, but I told them they could stop in front of The Beast, as we weren't planning to move.

When the couple introduced themselves, I said, "You've absolutely GOT TO get a vinylsun strip with your names on!"

I don't think I entirely suppressed my mirth.

"I know!" the lady replied. "We've not been together very long, but Wayne and Jayne? It's the biggest cliché in the world!"

My comment didn't seem to offend Jayne. She was from Burnley – a fellow Lancashire lass – so we were on the same wavelength. A characteristic inherited from my mother – that it's always worth it for the gag – made me question whether Mark and I ought to change our names to Wayne and Jayne, or something similar that would look good on a sun strip for The Beast.

As we chatted with Connie and Tom, Jayne and Wayne wandered into Ironbridge. They brought us a present from one of the many artisan shops that line the High Street. The orange and yellow Oriental garland complemented the rather understated interior décor of our truck perfectly. I could not get over their kindness.

Later, we walked into town with the pups. When I last saw the Iron Bridge around two decades ago, it was blue-grey. While carrying out an extensive restoration, English Heritage discovered its true colours. They repainted it in its original rusty red 'iron oxide' hue, similar to Scotland's iconic Forth Rail Bridge.

I love bridges anyway, but the one in Ironbridge is very special. As the world's first major cast iron bridge, it was revolutionary, and became a powerful symbol of the industrial revolution.

If you have ever had a split fireback in your fireplace, you will know that cast iron is a very brittle material. It has a low tensile strength, so it would be useless for a suspension-type bridge. But under compression, as in an arch, it is phenomenally strong.

Geography determined the bridge design. Rich deposits of iron, coal, clay, and limestone meant the area was already an industrial hub. A crossing of the River Severn in its steep-sided gorge would be a significant boost to local industry. However, the river's steep and unstable banks dictated the need for a single-span design. It also had to be high enough to allow ships to continue navigating the waterway, which was an important trading thoroughfare.

The trustees in charge of the development were sceptical about iron as a building material, and advertised for a stone, brick, or wood alternative. When they received no suitable plans, they accepted architect Thomas Pritchard's cast iron proposal. After two years of construction, the bridge opened in 1781. A testament to the success of its design is that, after a major flood in 1795, it was the only bridge left undamaged on the entire river.

To me, the Iron Bridge is a perfect merger of beauty and function. Five cast iron ribs form the 100 ft (30.5 m) arched span, with decorative rings and flourishes filling in the gaps. The structure comprises nearly 1,700 custom components, and approximately 385 tonnes of iron, all smelted and cast by Abraham Darby III at the Bedlam Furnaces. These, too, were revolutionary. They were the first blast furnaces in Britain to be built exclusively for smelting iron using coke, a process Darby pioneered. Coke is coal roasted without oxygen, which removes water, tar and other chemicals which would contaminate the iron. Previously, they smelted iron with charcoal as a source of heat and carbon. At the time, charcoal was scarce and expensive.

From the comfort of our bed, we could visualise the whole blast furnace process as we overlooked the site. Workers poured crushed limestone and ironstone (iron ore, full of iron oxides) in the chimney at the top. In the pot belly of the oven, blasts of air heated the coke to temperatures in excess of 3,600°F (2,000°C). This caused carbon in the coke to react with oxygen in the ore to create carbon dioxide and carbon monoxide gas, while leaving behind the iron. Calcium from the limestone removed impurities, such as silicates, from the ore, and formed the remaining slag.

As molten iron trickled out of the bottom of the blast furnace, workers drained it into moulds.

It was easy to imagine the noise, heat, fumes, and filth that would have surrounded the furnace. It must have been like Hell. Two artists, John Sell Cotman and Paul Sandby Munn are credited with naming it Bedlam. Originally, the term 'bedlam' referred to a psychiatric hospital in London, Saint Mary of Bethlehem – which dates back to at least the 1400s. Bethlehem morphed into Bethlem, then Bedlam; a word which later became synonymous with any scene of uproar, chaos, or confusion.

Sadly for us, this was perhaps prophetic.

I will always look back on Ironbridge so fondly.

We had a wonderful couple of days, filled with sun, fun, friend-ship, and beautiful walks through the dramatic gorge, but it definitely spelled an end to the good times.

Soon, bedlam would unfold in our lives when we drove The Beast up a mountain.

Chapter 26

Strife at Shooting Box

You cannot be serious! was a fair summation of my thoughts as my husband shoved a crumpled Ordnance Survey (OS) map onto my lap. As he stabbed his finger at his intended destination just prior to performing a U-turn with our lorry, I might even have exclaimed this out loud, and with some volume.

I had started to channel John McEnroe, the feisty tennis legend whose tantrums were as legendary as his topspin and trophies.

Mark had said, "We're going somewhere nice", but had omitted to fill in some essential details about our destination. Due to failures on the satnav front, he wanted me to navigate to the car park at Shooting Box via conventional means – i.e. using a paper map.

It might surprise you to learn that this was not the primary source of my discomfort. Even though the trusty satnav, with The Beast's immense dimensions and mass pre-programmed into it, had already led us up a tiny dead-end lane in the pleasant Shropshire village of Church Stretton and forced a cosy reverse.

When denied this particular path to pleasure, it circled back into the town centre and presented us with a three-tonne weight limit on The Burway, which is where you join us now, mid-U-turn once again.

I wasn't sorry that being a mere 12 tonnes overweight barred The Beast from The Burway. When I examined the route on the OS map, closely spaced arrows verified it was very steep (a 20% gradient), single track, and somewhat serpentine. Yet Mark's Plan C looked even more horrific.

That involved three sides of a square on slightly bigger roads. At first glance, it appeared more sensible; it was the ultimate section up to Shooting Box that prompted my outburst.

"That looks like a footpath to the top of a mountain!" I exclaimed.

Shooting Box car park was just short of the summit of an eminence known as the Long Mynd.

"It will be fine," Mark reassured me. "It's good practice for some of the roads we'll face when we drive to Mongolia!"

As I studied the map, I worried that Shropshire, a comfortable county in the heart of England, was already testing the limits of my bravery.

It was another 'interesting' run. As we passed small side lanes with no 'No HGV' signs, I felt slightly better. That obviously meant HGVs (Heavy Goods Vehicles) were welcome on the narrow country lanes we were weaving our way through.

At one point, we crossed a bridge with a maximum advisory vehicle length of 42.7 ft (13 m) and several 'Unsuitable for Caravans' signs. Since The Beast is only 10 metres long, it was absolutely fine – in a marginally terrifying way.

As we embarked upon the tortuous final section of track at Ratlinghope, with the right-hand edge of the carriageway abutting a steep drop, Mark asked,

"How are my wheels?"

The Beast is left-hand drive, which placed me firmly on the O.S.S. – the Oh Sh** Side. The one adjacent to the precipice. I craned out of the window and peered down.

"They're still on the road, if that's what you mean. But only just..."

The rim of The Beast's huge knobbly tyre overlapped the margins of the byway. A narrow cattle grid we had to pass through was simply an 'aim and hope'. I opened my eyes when our 8 ft (2.5 m) wide majesty sailed through the barriers on either side without impact, and the metal bars didn't collapse as we rattled across.

Not for the first time, we realised we couldn't underestimate truckin' with The Beast.

Journeys always took at least twice as long as planned. Driving such a large vehicle is like navigating through a maze full of dead-ends; limited at every turn by unexpected height and weight restrictions. Our trip from Wenlock Edge to Shooting Box was only supposed to be eight miles (12 km), but with satnav misdirections and this humongous detour, it took five hours. We didn't apply the brakes until 3 p.m.!

We gawped at the views as we walked the pooches. Sheep and wild ponies grazed among the moorland heather. Our little black girl, Lani, was not herself, so we didn't go too far, but the outlook in every direction blew us away. The Shropshire Hills richly deserve their designation as an Area of Outstanding Natural Beauty.

We cooked some chicken for Lani, but she wouldn't eat. She and Rosie, The Terrible Two, had raced around the woodland at our last stop, so we put it down to travelling, and assumed she would be better the next day. Our plan was the spectacular ten-mile (16 km) hike through Carding Mill Valley; listed among Britain's 'Hundred Best Walks'.

We parked right by a barrow; an ancient burial mound – and the only example of a disc barrow in Shropshire. Dated to nearly 2,000 B. C., the barrow had long outlasted the Shooting Box – a grouse-shooting hut that used to stand on the site.

As daylight faded, we were all alone on the moors, with no civilisation in sight. Thick cloud obscured the heavens – Shooting Box is a well-known star-gazing spot – but Mark still made me go outside purely to experience the rare sensation of total darkness!

It was late October, and all night, the wind howled and moaned around The Beast like the spirits of lost souls. Even so, I felt so cosy and content in our tiny cocoon. I only noticed the tight knot of anxiety in my stomach when it started to unravel, and I thought about how lucky we were to have everything we needed: warmth, shelter, food, companionship – the very seeds of happiness. I mused that perhaps this explains why people are so passionate about the time they spend in their caravans and motorhomes. Recreational vehicles spell unprecedented freedom, while paring life down to the simple necessities.

Unfortunately, in my experience, such moments of pure joy are often short-lived, and frequently prelude a catastrophe.

When we went to bed, Lani remained motionless on the sofa. This was unusual for a little girl who follows us to the loo at midnight, just to be close. I lifted her onto my pillow so she would feel loved and safe in the bosom of her family. She didn't move at all throughout the night. I was so worried I checked several times to make sure she was still breathing.

The following morning, we took the pups for a run to the viewpoint on the top of the Long Mynd. We got a few tuts from rufty-tufty ramblers with rucksacks and walking poles. The GORE-TEX brigade had clear opinions on Mark cradling Lani in his arms, and determined we needed to know.

"Fancy carrying a dog on a walk!" they scoffed, loud enough for us to hear. I couldn't bring myself to explain that normally, Lani has only two speeds: stop and supersonic. That no matter how many hours we were out, our pocket rocket would not stay still for a second, even if she was dragging along half a tree caught up in her tail.

At the cairn, I chatted with a couple of blokes who had stopped with a flask of coffee to enjoy the view.

"Shropshire is Britain's best-kept secret!" they told me. "Most people from 'down south' think it's just a made-up joke county, because it's the location of Blandings Castle in P.G. Wodehouse's *Jeeves and Wooster*!"

I saw what they meant. It was a sunny weekend, and there was hardly anyone there, with a surrounding panorama that was 360-degrees of magnificent.

To the east, they pointed out The Wrekin, the conical remains of an ancient volcano; the lengthy escarpment of Wenlock Edge; plus Cow Ridge and Haddon Hill catching the sun. To the west, they described the Stiperstones and its highest outcrop, the Devil's Chair, reputedly fly-tipped there by Lucifer himself. Curiously – so the legend goes – he dropped the stones out of his apron. Apparently, the strings broke while he was lugging them over from Ireland, and he couldn't be bothered to tidy up after himself. This struck me as odd. You'd think a pinny-wearing Prince of Darkness might adhere to higher standards of housekeeping.

In hot weather, legend claims the stones smell of brimstone, and on the longest night of the year, Old Nick returns to greet his followers, a bevy of spirits and witches, to appoint their king.

The chaps finished their virtual tour with two pub recommendations – The Ragleth and The Stiperstones Inns, as well as a quick mention that,

"On a clear day, you can see Snowdon!" – the highest peak in Wales.

I had no trouble visualising what poet A.E. Housman, author of *A Shropshire Lad*, was raving about when he spoke of his *Blue Remembered Hills*.

Into my heart an air that kills
From yon far country blows:
What are those blue remembered hills,
What spires, what farms are those?
That is the land of lost content,
I see it shining plain,
The happy highways where I went
And cannot come again.
A. E. Housman – *Public Domain*

When we got back, Lani ate a small amount of chicken and drank some water, which gave us hope, although she remained listless. It was Saturday morning, so we decided to forgo the joys of Carding Mill and the Long Mynd, and made a slightly hurried retrace of our precipitous route down the happy highways to attend an emergency vet appointment we secured at 2 p.m. in Shrewsbury.

The vet gave a swift diagnosis.

"She has a temperature, so she's telling us she's fighting off infection. I'll give her an anti-inflammatory, which will act really quickly."

The injection did the trick. At 4 p.m. and 6 p.m., she ate a little more chicken, so we thought she was out of the woods. But by morning, she was lethargic again, and incredibly hot.

Our pups always seem to get sick at weekends. Since it was Sunday, we called our own vet in Bournemouth. When we explained Lani's symptoms, they advised not to wait until Monday to have her seen. Our options were limited, so after a frantic internet search, we did a mercy dash at The Beast's top speed of 45 mph (72 kph) to the only emergency vet we could find open, at Cheltenham Racecourse.

I dampened Lani's fur to keep down her temperature, but I had a bad feeling as we drove through Herefordshire and Worcestershire into Gloucestershire. The whole way was littered with something I had never seen before – billboard after billboard advertising a pet crematorium.

"Her temperature is 40°C (104°F)! I think we'd better keep her in," the vet said. I will never forget Lani's forlorn little face as the vet took her away from us, as limp as a rag doll. Sad puppydog eyes caught mine with an expression of shock and betrayal.

The veterinary facilities at the racecourse were second to none, and the animal hospital had its own pathology department on site. This gave us the blessing of an almost immediate diagnosis.

An hour later, the vet rang and said,

"Lani's blood results show her organs are all okay, but she's battling an infection. That is why her white cell neutrophil count is very low. It's 0.4. An immunosuppressed dog on chemotherapy would be 1.5, so she is very much at risk of sepsis. We have put her on a drip and intravenous antibiotics. We're trying to get a urine sample to rule out a urinary infection, but she's so dehydrated she's absorbing all the fluid. She's comfortable and sleeping, and not in any danger."

I suspected the reassurance was all bedside manner. The vet had been very sympathetic to her previous customer.

"I'm so sorry for your loss," she'd whispered as a lady carried out a tiny bundle, wrapped in a blanket.

My heart broke for her.

An emergency appointment had undoubtedly been the correct course of action for Lani. A delay could have been fatal, but what followed was the most drawn-out night. The lack of one small black dog leaves an unfeasibly large gap in your life – and in your bed. Neither Mark nor I could contain our sobs.

During fitful bouts of sleep, I dreamed that I was in a museum and could see Lani's face underneath the display cabinets. She was okay, but faint, and out of reach behind the glass.

As a scientist, I don't really believe in such things, but sometimes, I do wonder if I might be a witch! I am from Lancashire – that famous witches' county – after all.

Frequently, I voice Mark's thoughts, however random, as if I've read his mind. I also get premonitions. An incident that particularly sticks with me took place years ago, just before my brother left to drive back to university after the holidays. I felt an overpowering sense of dread as I hugged him and said goodbye. Thirty minutes later, when the phone rang, I knew instantly it was him, and that things were not okay.

He'd been in a car accident. Thankfully, although the car was a write-off, he was unhurt. Still, I have never forgotten the weirdness of knowing with such certainty something I could never have known.

Unfortunately, my psychic superpowers have yet to yield any really beneficial premonitions, like any details of what is actually going to happen – or the winning Lottery numbers!

With Lani, I experienced an overwhelming sense that she would pull through. I told Mark, but almost didn't dare to hope. The omen of the pet crematorium haunted me. Then, as we were walking our seven-year-old pups in Cheltenham's Pittville Park, a lady shared that her five-year-old King Charles Spaniel, Boris, had died of liver failure.

"Although Dragon Vets were excellent," she assured us, not very reassuringly, when we told her the reason behind our visit to Cheltenham.

The following day, we called Dragon the moment they opened at

8.30 a.m. Reception said,

"The vets haven't done their rounds yet, but Lani is stable and having a cuddle with the nurse."

The vet didn't return our call until 12.30 p.m., four hours later. Mark and I were in pieces.

"Lani's had an ultrasound and X-ray, and is doing well. We'll keep her on fluids for the afternoon, but she's eaten, and she can come home this evening. We'll book you a discharge appointment with Alan at 6.15."

It was the best news and the most interminable wait. Less positive was the bill, although if a four-figure sum gave us back our baby girl, we didn't care. We had pre-paid some money on account, as we don't have pet insurance. It's too expensive for four dogs, particularly as they age, and gives only limited cover. Veterinary treatment is also much more reasonably priced abroad. When we first adopted our furry family, we made the decision to take any veterinary expenses on the chin, but as I told the vet,

"We'd re-mortgage the house for her if we had to!"

Without treatment, she would have died. What better cause to spend money on than saving a life? I was just so glad we could do this for her.

When we picked her up, Alan explained she'd had a bladder infection. He'd noticed some ammonium bi-urate crystals in her urine, which may have been an anomaly of the test, but could also be a sign of a very rare genetic disorder. He was aware of this condition because as luck would have it, he had dealt with it before.

"We can't test for it while she's on antibiotics. Your own vet will be able to run the analysis, although it has to be done quickly, because the crystals can form in the sample as soon as it is taken."

She needed a check-up in a few days, but I knew then that we would return to Cheltenham for Alan to perform the test. Our vets are great, but don't have labs on site and may not have Alan's experience of Lani's condition. Our beloved fur baby would receive only the best and most expert care. In any case, other than the obvious, we had enjoyed our stay in Cheltenham. Our park-up was glorious; right next to Pittville Park, and within walking distance of the town centre. We had made friends with a whole selection of dog walkers, all of whom kept returning to The Beast to ask about Lani.

Other than it being the land of lost content for both us and Housman, we had found Shropshire (and Gloucestershire) to be incredibly friendly counties, but most importantly, we would not be taking any chances with our precious wee pup!

It was such a tonic to see Lani back in action, chasing squirrels and racing around with Rosie; The Terrible Two reunited. Her tummy and legs were shaved, and she tired quickly, but otherwise, she was none the worse for her ordeal.

Unfortunately, though, this wasn't the end of our troubles.

Who knew what strife a flat leisure battery might lead to...?

Chapter 27

Sinkhole.Tiles.Sorted. - How To Get Stuck in a Go-Anywhere Truck!

B ack in Stratford-upon-Avon, as the crowds mobbed our rig at the Adventure Overland Show, the watchword was, "That's definitely a 'Go-Anywhere' truck!"

With four-wheel drive, the ability to climb slopes up to sixty-degrees, and anecdotal assurance that, "You could drive that on the moon!" we had absolute faith in the capabilities of our 15-tonne beauty, The Beast.

We also had 1300 watts of solar panels on our roof.

The electrician who fitted it dismissed our questions about fitting a battery-to-battery charger to replenish our bank of leisure batteries as we drove. He assured us, "With that lot up top, you could power a rock festival!"

But as the bright October days shortened, we realised he was referring to summer festivals only. We were starting to use more energy than we generated. Our AGM (Absorbent Glass Mat) gel batteries dwindled to 10 volts; a level that could damage them permanently. We desperately needed an electrical hook-up.

The campground in Cheltenham was full, which wasn't too convenient. Although she was home after her near-death experience, Lani had to return to the vet in Cheltenham for a check-up the next day. That left no choice but to move to a campsite further away. Who knew what contention this would throw up?

We have a history with cornfields.

In Romania, our satnav led us, caravan and all, across two cornfields. The definition of what constitutes a road in Romania is a bit more malleable than in the rest of Europe. We didn't expect to encounter such difficulties in Gloucestershire!

The satnav took us blithely into a lane that declared itself 'Unsuitable for Heavy Goods Vehicles'. Such signs are often advisory. My dad frequently used a byway whose sign asserted it 'Unsuitable for Motors'. It was such a common shortcut that, as kids, we often asked, "Are we going down 'The Unsuitable'?"

And at this point in our trucking career, Mark and I were still riding the wave of invincibility endowed by the possession of a 'Go-Anywhere' truck.

As he turned the wheel, I chortled. "We drove up to Shooting Box, which was virtually on the summit of a mountain!"

I mean, how bad could it be?

The encroaching boughs of mature trees started to meet above the narrow road. As they scraped along the roof and sides of The Beast, icy fingers of doubt began to creep into my mind. When the darkening green tunnel drew us down a single-track decline as steep as Hickstead's infamous Derby Bank, I lost my bottle.[1]

I was following our journey on the map, and said to Mark, "This road is about five miles long. What if it gets worse? I saw a sign back there that said the village it passes through is particularly unsuitable for HGVs."

As Franklin D. Roosevelt observed in 1932, there is nothing to fear but fear itself.

Because fear is contagious.

Looking at the sharp downhill and the invading branches, Mark's faith deserted him too. We had gone much too far to reverse out, so we looked in vain for somewhere to turn around. When we eventually spotted two field entrances opposite each other, slightly offset and at completely the wrong angle, we were desperate. We jumped at it because it appeared to be our only option.

Mark reversed into the access on the left, ready to pull forward into the one almost opposite. Instantly, The Beast's 15-tonne majesty sank immovably into Gloucestershire.

My heart and stomach followed in quick succession.

In a moment, our plight had transitioned from a slightly tricky situation into serious trouble. I jumped out of the cab to see four huge ridged drive tyres spinning in a rusty-red soup of slippery, sticky clay.

---

1. Hickstead's infamous Derby Bank is one of showjumping's most famous – and feared – fences. It comprises a 10 ft 6 in (3.2 m) drop straight after a jump. Without a precise approach, disaster awaits...

"We're supposed to be able to ascend a sixty-degree gradient!" I squeaked as I looked at the tiny incline.

Mark and I took stock. The cloying mud clung to the soles of our trainers. As we slid about in the manner of newborn giraffes making their *Dancing on Ice* debut, we identified the problem. Without traction, a 'Go-Anywhere' truck goes nowhere – not even on the flat. On slick tyres, even 275 horsepower and four-wheel drive were not sufficient to propel The Beast up a shallow rise and over the two-inch (5 cm) tarmac lip bordering the road.

In times of trouble, I am driven to investigate all avenues and proffer unwelcome advice.

"Why don't you try the diff lock?" I said.

This feature of a four-wheel-drive vehicle allows each wheel to act independently. If one is spinning, the others can still rotate normally and utilise their grip to push the vehicle forwards. It made no difference. All four drive wheels were spinning.

I followed a track that led downhill through the cornfield, but saw it didn't rejoin the road at the bottom. We didn't want to get ourselves further downhill in a muddy field, and further into trouble.

I sensed a husbandly eruption brewing and executed a tactical retreat. In times of stress, Mark doesn't always appreciate my contributions. One woman's 'help' is another man's 'interference', so I left him rummaging for the sand ladders, or 'waffle boards' that enable the tyres to grip on slippery surfaces. He'd buried them in the deepest depths of The Beast's expansive garage, because why would we need them in Gloucestershire? To reach them, he had to unload the bikes from their rack, then decant most of our windsurfing gear straight into the mud.

It was another useful lesson – stow your recovery equipment where it's easily accessible.

Of course, I sensed this wasn't the ideal moment to point this out to Mark.

It was difficult for me just to sit in the cab doing nothing, with four scared pups and the branch of a blackthorn bush poking in through the driver's side window. The blackthorn was heavy with juicy ripe sloe berries, but I could not muster the enthusiasm to think about them, never mind harvest them. Despite the fact that homemade sloe gin is one of my favourite things – cherry-red, bittersweet and almost vaporous on my palate...

A fortifying nip of alcohol – or maybe a few bottles – would have been most welcome in our current predicament, but there were more pressing matters to consider. I cogitated how we might get a 15-tonne truck out of a muddy field. Lani had to return to the vet's the following day. I supposed we might hire a car, but that would mean leaving our home and all our possessions bogged down in somebody's field.

Crouch's was a lorry recovery company, but could a suitably powerful recovery vehicle even reach us down the lane? And first things first. To summon recovery or a hire car, how would we give our location? Other than 'in a cornfield down an unnamed road somewhere between Cheltenham and Cirencester,' we had no idea where we were.

I was still getting to grips with apps. I knew of one called What3Words, which pinpoints your location anywhere on earth to within a three-metre square. I'd noted it as potentially handy for back-country skiing or hiking emergencies, but as with Park4Night, because I'd never needed it, I hadn't bothered to check it out.

So, while Mark slithered around in a lake of terracotta-coloured clay, surrounded by our mud-caked possessions, I decided the moment had come to achieve What3Words mastery. While keeping one eye open for any passing farmers who might have a big tractor, of course.

Mark prised the muck out of the tyre treads with our much prized and newly acquired Trilex tyre lever. Then, he placed a hard-won sand ladder on the ground in front of each of the rear drive wheels. After an hour of hard labour, The Beast lurched forward in three short bursts of three feet (1 m); the length of a sand ladder. After each brief but hope-infused advance, we levered a mud-encrusted waffle board out of the ground and moved it forward to the front of each wheel. Yet, the mass of relief that flooded into me as our drive wheels gripped tarmac evaporated just as quickly when Mark drove slightly uphill into the field entrance opposite.

He was still determined to do a U-turn, even when I told him, "I checked the onward route on the map while you were getting out the sand ladders. There is a way to avoid the village and rejoin the main road."

I stayed outside with a walkie talkie to guide him backwards, while scanning the lane for traffic. A grassy bank about three feet high stood in the way of him reversing around the corner. Our 'Go-Anywhere' truck mounted it, then promptly froze, motionless. Her engine roared and screeched, as two drive wheels hovered, useless, in midair.

Then, her weight shifted. The grounded wheels slipped. Fifteen tonnes of rolling steel slithered down the bank and bounced back down onto *terra firma* with a gut-churning lurch to the left. I looked on, helpless, as this forced The Beast's front wheels onto yet another slimy patch of mud and her nose slewed downhill. The smell of wet earth and diesel fumes filled the air, and my mouth was as dry as Death Valley. Every hammering heartbeat convinced me that my home, which contained everything I loved, was about to overturn.

I had been so relieved to escape the first field. Now, the nightmare had not only re-started, it had upped its game. I couldn't bring myself to take photos or film this unfolding disaster.

Mark was unable to steer around the bank, which ruled out any hope of a *volte-face*. One small consolation was that in our latest muddy field, gravity was on our side, rather than working against us.

Inch by inch, with tyres squelching, Mark reversed down the incline, and rejoined the road, facing the same direction as before. I pleaded with him just to carry on down the hill on the paved road.

After this second foray into a field, our tyres were once again coated with slime. To clear the treads, Mark jerked the steering wheel from left to right in the narrow confines of the lane. With telltale double arrows, the map warned of the hill's killer gradient. With our goo-filled tyres, I was terrified we would simply slide straight down it, like an oversized, NATO-green toboggan.

Once we reached the campsite, I was ready to weep with relief. Mark resembled a mud-caked gargoyle, and I felt hollow and depleted. At least it gave us a chance to charge up our batteries – and launder our filthy clothes.

We both felt ridiculous for getting our 'Go-Anywhere' truck stuck, but that in itself was an important lesson.

Even 'Go-Anywhere' trucks have limitations!

We could thank the gods it happened in a country where help was readily available in our native language. In addition, we'd proven our ability to self-rescue, using those pieces of equipment you carry but hope never to use.

Over a home-cooked lamb curry, we reflected on how a single, insignificant problem has a talent for cascading into a full-blown crisis. It was a perfect example of chain theory, in which one minor event can swiftly precipitate an improbable series of consequences. Chain theory lies behind many of the world's disasters.

In our case, the inciting incident was trusting our electrician when he assured us that so much solar made a battery-to-battery charger superfluous.

This design flaw compelled us to find a campsite, because our batteries had run low. The nearest site in Cheltenham was full, forcing us to Cirencester. We usually checked the satnav's chosen route on a map or Google Earth, but stressed and upset because of Lani's near-death scare, we omitted this crucial step. So, we got bogged down in a field, with the added pressure of a deadline to get our precious darling back to the vet.

If only we'd taken the advice from the Overland Show and stopped for a cup of tea before our dash to Cirencester.

At least I found some humour in the situation as I told Mark the name of our What3Words' location.

"It was Sinkhole.Tiles.Sorted. If you think of sand ladders as tiles, that is the whole sorry tale abridged ironically into three words!"

We both hoped that our horrible week was over, but sadly, life is never that simple. We and our recovery gear had not yet escaped the murky mires of Gloucestershire.

The following morning, as we rushed to pack up and get Lani to her vet appointment, a couple approached us.

"Our motorhome is stuck in the mud. Can you tow us off?"

Like good Samaritans, we made time for them, despite our deadline. They were in the same position as we had been yesterday – wheels skidding in a sea of red mud. We were embarrassed to confess our tribulations from the previous day, but we thought it might make them feel better. They were gobsmacked.

"What? You got THAT stuck! Surely, it's a 'Go-Anywhere' truck..."

The rescue didn't take long. We had a kinetic recovery rope and a whole array of shackles – now stored in an easily accessible location!

They thanked us profusely, and we all went on our way.

Half an hour later, I received a phone call.

"Can I call you back? We're driving, and I can't hear you over the engine noise."

"It's urgent."

"Okay. Hang on a second and we'll find somewhere to pull over."

I thought it might be the vet, so it came as a shock to discover an irate campsite owner on the other end of the line.

"You've caused damage to our campsite and driven off without saying anything!"

"I wasn't aware that we'd caused any damage," I said, perplexed, "and we certainly wouldn't have driven off if we knew we had. If we have damaged anything, we're sorry, and we will certainly pay for it."

"You've damaged our grass and knocked over a post. You should know better than to drive a vehicle like yours on the grass after all the rain we've had lately!"

"We didn't drive over the grass. We were careful to stay on the tarmac. If we caused any damage, I'm sorry, but we didn't notice."

"You can't possibly have not noticed!"

His tone was beginning to raise my hackles, but I remained calm as I reiterated my position.

"We didn't drive on the grass, and we didn't notice any damage. As I said, if we had, we would not have driven off."

He followed the same circular argument for several minutes. He repeated his accusations; I apologised, but unfortunately, the stress of the last few days caught up with me and eventually, he pushed me too far.

I lost my cool.

"Okay. You're accusing me of being *dishonest* by driving off; *lying* about damage I didn't realise we'd caused; and being *stupid* by saying we should know better than to drive on grass, which we didn't! Let me get this straight. What we did was a good turn. For you, and for a couple who asked us to tow them off because they were stuck on their pitch. We could have done without it, because have a vet appointment in Cheltenham. As I said, we'll pay for any damage we've caused. That's what you're getting at, isn't it? You want money out of us." My voice started to achieve the soprano frequency of a fishwife. I concluded hysterically with, "My dog nearly died two days ago. We're on the way to the vet, and YOU are delaying us."

As I hung up, I unleashed a scream of pure, unfiltered frustration and anguish. I'm not sure the telephone had fully disconnected. But I hoped he heard it. The sonic evidence of my outrage over his bloody grass, a toppled pole, and the fact he couldn't confirm whether it was split, or fixable, or how much it would cost to put right.

Somehow, I had restrained myself from retorting that if anyone was stupid, it was him. After all – HE should have known better than to site a motorhome on a grass pitch after all the rain...

Now, however, I'd made up my mind.

In light of his appalling attitude, I would not be paying for anything unless he proved beyond doubt we were responsible. And that would take some effort, because I had no intention of responding to any further communications.

From my polite apology and offer to pay for reparations, he had really turned the situation around!

I saved his number under a rude name, so that we would have prior warning if he called, but he didn't contact us again. Either he heard me howl like a banshee and experienced remorse for causing such pain and distress, or more likely decided he was dealing with a complete lunatic, and thought it best to let it go.

I suspect he simply wanted to vent his anger on somebody about the muddy mess the motorhome made while trying to exit his pitch – which was nothing to do with us.

The whole experience reminded me why we prefer to avoid campsites. The greater the separation between us and petty-minded jobsworths, the better.

Back at our free-and-easy park-up in Cheltenham, our new doggie walking friends all greeted us warmly and asked after Lani. She sailed through her check-up, and the vet returned our mischievous little minx with a clean bill of health.

However, one last catastrophe awaited us.

As yet, we knew nothing of it, but it was ticking like a time bomb.

When it finally went off, it would spell an abrupt and unwelcome end to our travels.

Note: I have changed the What3Words location name ever-so-slightly while keeping the sense, to avoid being pursued by another irate citizen of Gloucestershire for driving on his grass!

Chapter 28

Painswick Dog Pie & The Source of the Thames

F rom Cheltenham to Painswick was fewer than a dozen miles, but the satnav seemed to be acting out a personal vendetta. It decided there was some reason to avoid the main A46, which neatly joined the two. Instead, it shunted us through the mayhem of the Gloucester ring road, then spat us into a maze of winding lanes. Maybe it was bored. Maybe it wanted to test our mettle. Either way, we had slightly clenched teeth, buttocks, and frayed tempers by the time we rumbled into the village.

Painswick itself is absurdly pretty. It is much less touristed than fellow Cotswold darlings such as Broadway or Bourton-on-the-Water. Although dubbed 'Queen of the Cotswolds', Painswick wears her crown quietly.

One of England's earliest wool towns, Painswick built her prosperity on fleeces and weaving. Towering facades of pale gold limestone jostled for space, their eaves almost brushing the roadway. Huddled between them, a distinctive black and white half-timbered gable dating from 1428 is the oldest building in England to house a post office.

Once, most attic rooms rattled with looms, and we soon discovered that weaving remained an unspoken motif. Lines of parked cars on the impossibly narrow high street contributed a delightful frisson of hysteria to the joy of threading The Beast through. Our manoeuvres demanded dexterity equal to firing one's flying shuttle through warp and weft.

As the view suddenly opened out, the slender and elegant limestone spire of St. Mary's Church shone in the sunlight. It contrasted beautifully with its surrounding oasis of emerald green. The square tower, topped by its fine steeple, rises 262 ft (80 m). It houses 14 bells – an unusually grand number for a parish church – and a feature that makes it beloved of campanologists. However, as we approached, bell ringing was furthest from our minds.

Parking was impossible.

Mark had to stay with the truck, shuffling around the busy car park to let vehicles come and go, while I slid out of the cab to undertake a fleeting solo visit.

"I'll take lots of photos for you," I promised, "so you'll *feel* you've been there...!"

In 1086, the Domesday Book mentioned a church at Painswick, although the present building is far newer, originating from around 1377. The church is a stunner, but its churchyard really steals your breath. Spread over two acres, it brims with elaborate tabletop, chest, and 'tea caddy' tombs, fashioned from the same luminous stone as the cottages and church. They date from the early 1600s, and many are the handiwork of local stonemason, John Bryan. His creations went way beyond the typical styles of the time, and his grand edifices commemorate the town's wealthy merchants, clothiers, and associated businesspeople.

Fittingly, Bryan lies beneath the most striking tomb of all – a sharp, angular pyramid, which was startlingly unusual for the 17th century. Exotic, bold, and unapologetically different, it evokes the monumental grandeur of Giza – or given its dimensions, perhaps even pyramids found at Meroe in Sudan. All in a quiet Cotswold village, centuries before Napoleon Bonaparte's 19th century invasion of Egypt sparked a Europe-wide fascination for Egyptology.

I could really identify with Bryan's bold statement of individuality and ambition among his more conventional neighbours.

Yet it's not only the tombs that make St. Mary's so unforgettable. Ninety-nine yew trees, trained and clipped into bulbous lollipops, pompoms, or umbrella-like domes, line the paths. Like immaculate sentries, they guard the dead and shade the ornate sarcophagi. Legend insists that it's impossible to count the trees – you will always come to a different total. It also claims the Devil himself would never allow a hundredth tree to survive... That said, the extra yew donated by the Diocese of Gloucester for the Millennium is not merely alive but thriving – in full defiance of Old Nick's restrictive arboreal practices.

I don't blame Lucifer for lowering his tally book. The overall effect of dark sculpted yew set against vivid grass and ornate, sunlit stone was so arresting, I could believe it might cause Beelzebub to lose count.

Yet when I entered the church from the peaceful serenity of the churchyard, I sensed the press of history and the heartbeat of old turmoil.

During the first English Civil War (1642–45), nearby Gloucester was the strategic key to the upper Severn valley. It was a small but stubborn stronghold for Oliver Cromwell's Parliamentarians (Roundheads).

Royalist troops – the Cavaliers, who were loyal to King Charles I – dominated the surrounding area.

The Cavaliers pulled St. Mary's Church into the conflict by using it as a makeshift prison when they besieged Gloucester. The siege collapsed on 5th September 1643 when the Parliamentarian Earl of Essex attacked the Royalist army that encircled Gloucester. They retreated to regroup and spent a night in Painswick. Tradition holds that the King himself climbed Painswick Beacon and declared, "This must be paradise." The name stuck, and the hamlet at the foot of the hill is still called Paradise.

Yet St. Mary's Civil War stories aren't just told in guidebooks or on plaques – they are literally gouged into the walls. Scratches and scars left by soldiers and prisoners bear witness to that moment in history. Inside, the nave was dim and hushed, but one piece of graffiti stopped me in my tracks. On the last pillar on the left-hand side before the pulpit, Richard Foot, a captive Parliamentarian soldier, had carved his signature and a single resonant line from Spenser's epic allegorical poem *The Faerie Queene.*

"Be bold, be bold, but not too bold..."

I read his words with a jolt.

In the ballad, an enchantress inscribed the phrase above a doorway. They urge the heroine, Britomart, to summon the courage to proceed – but not to the point of reckless destruction. I wondered about Richard Foot's message to history while trapped by the chaos of war. Was it his personal motto? Or perhaps a note to self to ward off the despair of incarceration? Was it a warning to Cromwell – or a defiant taunt to his captors? Or possibly a motivational appeal to his fellow soldiers to steel themselves for hardship, but caution against overreach?

I traced the uneven letters with my fingertips, and for a moment, the centuries fell away. Richard's voice could have been whispering through the stone, sending his almost four-hundred-year-old words of prudence and wisdom directly to Mark and me.

We'd been bold – we'd cast ourselves loose from a 'normal' life. We'd quit lucrative careers and pinned our hopes of happiness on an oversized and contrary vintage truck. The Beast had tested us every step of the way. Converting her into our home had already tried our courage to breaking point, and she appeared determined to continue the challenge.

Outside, Bryan's pyramid seemed to me as much a message in stone as Richard Foot's graffiti. It was proof that even a simple shape could thumb its nose at convention. As I stood between the two, I couldn't help feeling they were both still speaking. Here, in this quiet corner of a medieval church, as our life teetered on the threshold between bravery and folly, the voices of a mason and a veteran soldier carried the same lesson we needed for our own journey with The Beast.

That courage is vital, but so is knowing when to ease off on the throttle.

***

Our departure from Painswick was less than dignified.

With The Beast wedged, like an ill-tempered bullock in a castrating pen, we resorted to walkie-talkies and an elaborate reverse shuffle to exit the cramped car park.

After the morning's tribulations, I was gagging for a cup of tea and something to eat, but there was no opportunity to linger. It was a shame, since Thomas Twining, who founded the famous tea merchants in 1706, was one of Painswick's sons. We had no chance to sample Painswick's Bow Wow Sauce, or Puppy Dog Pie – the traditional fare of the Clypping ceremony on Feast Sunday, celebrated on the first Sabbath to fall after 19th September. Clypping derives from the Anglo-Saxon *clyppan*, meaning to 'clasp' or 'hug', and refers to a circle of youngsters with flowers in their hair surrounding the church in a living embrace. Followed, of course, by feasting, drinking, disorderly conduct – and a spot of Dog Pie.

The roots of this curious tradition lie in a muddle of folk tales. Each proposes a far-fetched circumstance that might have led to man's best friend being swapped for more traditional pie fillings.

Thankfully, Painswick's poochy pies and other canine-sounding delicacies contain no real dog. Rather, the pie has small porcelain puppies baked inside. Similar to a sixpence in a Christmas pudding, it's considered a token of luck to find one – so long as you don't break your teeth on it.

The China figurines seem to be the most important ingredient, since I found references to dog pie containing anything from plums to meat – hopefully more mutton than mutt.

Happily, there's no such canine controversy over Painswick's Bow Wow (or Wow Wow) Sauce. That is simply port, wine vinegar, pickled walnuts, fiery English mustard, and mushroom ketchup blended with beef stock and thickened with a buttery roux. It was originally cooked up as an accompaniment for meat by William Kitchener, a 19th-century celebrity chef who invented potato crisps! (At least he was the first to write down the recipe for deep fried potato shavings in his bestselling book *The Cook's Oracle*.) I'm not sure why it's called Bow Wow Sauce, although it makes a guest appearance in William Black's gastronomic quest *The Land that Thyme Forgot*. Black links it with one of Painswick's outlandish dog pie legends. After coming to blows with their neighbours from Stroud, Black suggests the villagers of Painswick served Bow Wow Sauce at a reconciliatory feast as atonement for feeding them a pie filled with real puppies...

Fans of Terry Pratchett's *Discworld* will also have heard about Wow Wow Sauce, although Terry's recipe differs slightly because he incorporates sulphur and saltpetre, which make it an altogether more explosive concoction. Pratchett ranks it among the world's most dangerous condiments – second only to Three Mile Island Dressing.

Obviously, the nuclear option.

***

The next leg of our trip should have been simple.

But naturally, the road was closed, which necessitated a second long and labyrinthine diversion. Every corner revealed another impatient driver in a Range Rover, puffed up with horsepower and self-importance. As we duelled for dominance in the hedge-pinched Cotswold lanes, they glared at us as if we'd purchased an oversized, overpowered juggernaut purely to ruin their afternoon – and upstage them by bringing a bigger toy to their playground.

Laurie Lee, who drank his cider with Rosie in these hills, was born in the nearby village of Slad. It would have been a perfect literary detour, and an opportunity to raise a glass – figuratively at least – to another English writer whose words have become part of the landscape. But the thought of shoehorning The Beast into yet another constricted Cotswold car park made us blanch. We'd had our fill of botty-clenching squeezes – and our puppies deserved a run.

On the map, the lay-by at Kemble looked ideal. It was right on the Thames Path, a stone's throw from the river's source. On arrival, however, the reality was that a narrow, muddy, and potholed lay-by marked the birthplace of England's most famous river. The ground sloped so much the truck listed like a grounded ship, threatening to roll gently into the hedge.

"Mark, I saw a flat lay-by further back on the road..." I said.

So we retreated there for a brew and a quiet audit of our questionable decisions.

By now it was 3:30 p.m. and besides being ravenously hangry and gagging for a cuppa, I felt we'd wasted a glorious sunny day. It was perfect for a doggie walk, although the wind was Arctic... Thus, our sartorial judgment to wear shorts was not the only thing we called into question.

Here we were, near a trickle in a field destined to become the mighty waterway that is England's most famous river. But similar to us, it was swamped in chaos and grime, with only a promise of better things ahead.

We abandoned the idea and changed our plans.

We set course for Malmesbury, hoping it might offer redemption.

Chapter 29

Malmesbury: A Flying Monk, A Fallen Spire, & England's Forgotten Capital

M almesbury, a small, unassuming Wiltshire market town, isn't the sort of destination most people put on their bucket list.

It's quaint enough: perched on a hill encircled almost fully by two tributaries of the River Avon, and it has a few distinguishing features. Although it started life as an Iron Age fort, the ruins of a once-mighty Benedictine abbey now crown the peak, while its 15th-century octagonal market cross looks like a Gothic gazebo on steroids. It's elaborately carved, and has eight pillars and eight arches holding up a vaulted roof, but no one knows who commissioned it, or who stumped up the cash for it – or why.

But blink, and you'd miss it.

Had it not been a convenient place to stop on our route home, like most, we would have simply passed Malmesbury by.

Yet scratch the surface – or more precisely, get up close and personal with the Abbey's weathered stones – and you'll find a town that was once England's first capital, a centre of learning and pilgrimage, and a stage for war, science, and disaster. A place where hidden histories hide in plain sight.

And as we discovered, it's also a place where park-ups hide in plain sight.

A wrong turn trapped us in a Co-op's compact parking lot. Unable to enter because we were mid-manoeuvre, a woman thoughtfully abandoned her car on the bend opposite – thus ensuring that we had no chance to leave and make room for her. Nevertheless, there's always an upside. While we waited for her to shift, I raced into the shop to buy wine.

Then we followed the signs for long-term parking. This was a smart move, since that was where we wanted to go – contrary to the satnav's stubborn insistence on routing us to a mystery destination conjured up by its own deranged imaginings.

We left The Beast in a car park by a weir on the river and took the dogs for a run along a nearby footpath. It led to the cricket club, near where Mark declared a large gravel area inviting. I pleaded with him not to relocate The Beast.

"Mark, the access is up a steep, unmetalled road, and there are low trees..."

A niggling twinge in my lower back was already registering its objections to six-hours in the passenger seat. You might think being chauffeured at a leisurely pace along scenic country roads sounds relaxing, but think again! They don't design army trucks for comfort. My pew – a hard wooden bench seat upholstered in mottled green vinyl with neither seatbelt nor suspension – presses my coccyx into service as a rudimentary seismograph. My *derrière* presents the first line of detection for every minor tremor, while an unexpected pothole or invisible speed ramp catapults me into orbit! Plus, following the calamitous events of the previous few days, my adventure cup was very much overflowing.

When Mark agreed, my sigh of relief could have powered the Dogger Bank Wind Farm.

It was a golden October evening, so on a musky carpet of fallen leaves from the stately trees that lined the damp, earthy pathway, we clambered upwards to explore the town.

Malmesbury is England's oldest borough. In the 10th century, Athelstan, Alfred the Great's grandson and the first king of a unified England, declared it his capital. Reputedly, he is buried within the Abbey, although the 15th-century tomb dedicated to him is empty of relics.

It's possible his grave was moved to avoid desecration by the Normans, so like Richard III, Athelstan is another lost king.

The footpath led straight to the Abbey, whose arches and pinnacles dominated the skyline. Bathed in late summer sunshine, the whole soaring edifice glowed with the warm ochre hue of intense English mustard. As we dithered about with four dogs, admiring flying buttresses and the fine Norman carvings on the porticoes that framed the south porch, a chap passing by with a plastic bag full of shopping stopped to ask if we were okay.

When we said we were just having a look around, he introduced himself as Mike and treated us to an impromptu tour!

"The Abbey used to be twice this size," Malmesbury's proud resident revealed, "and it had the highest steeple in Europe. It was over 430 ft (130 m), which is 23 ft (7 m) taller than Salisbury Cathedral's. That's really something, because Salisbury is *still* the UK's tallest!

"But around 1500, a thunderstorm brought it down. They say the lightning bolt instantly turned water in the stone to steam, so the masonry beneath the wooden steeple literally exploded. The collapse took half the building with it. Local lore claims the golden ball from the top rolled down the high street as far as the George Inn!"

He gestured toward a lone church spire across the road. "That's all that's left of St. Paul's parish church. After Henry VIII dissolved the monasteries, the Abbey became the main place of worship. It's still the parish church today.

"So Malmesbury is very curious. It has an abbey with no steeple facing a steeple with no church!"

I remembered that St. Mary's in Painswick had lost her spire to a lightning strike in 1883, but that wasn't all the two towns had in common. Mike beckoned us toward the smooth stonework of the south face and pointed out the most fascinating feature of all. One we could so easily have missed.

"Do you see all these dings and pockmarks? They were made by musket balls. Malmesbury was a Cavalier (Royalist) stronghold during the Civil War, but fighting was fierce. Between 1644 and 1646, the town changed hands *seven* times. The resisting forces used the Abbey as a fortress. They mounted a cannon on the west tower and fired down Abbey Row. The west tower is no longer there. It collapsed eventually, perhaps due to battle damage.

"When Malmesbury finally fell, the stories say the victors lined up the leaders of the resistance against the Abbey walls and executed them by firing squad."

We looked at the pattern of the musket fire. A neat constellation in one area certainly suggested something more than random crossfire. I shivered as I ran my hand over the scarred stone, humbled by the dead weight of events that took place there. Under my fingers was another ghostly reminder of how bitterly our nation once fought over its future, and how those brutal struggles shaped the identity of the country we know today.

Mike nodded west towards Abbey Row, where another survivor of Malmesbury's turbulent past is still open for business.

"If you go out that way, you'll pass The Old Bell Hotel, England's oldest purpose-built hotel. The monks established it as the Abbey guest house in 1220 on the foundations of Malmesbury Castle – which is why it was called The Castle Inn for many years. The monks didn't approve of the castle because Bishop Roger of Salisbury built it when he seized the Abbey and deposed the abbot! So they pulled it down.

"The Old Bell's guest list wasn't too shabby. Henry II and his future Archbishop of Canterbury, Thomas Becket, stayed in the original castle. When it became a guest house, Henry III visited three times, and in the late 1400s, during the Wars of the Roses, King Edward IV lodged there on his way to the Battle of Tewkesbury. Although the Abbey was dissolved in 1539, the hotel carried on – and eight hundred years later, it's still doing the same!"

Just before Mike left, he shared his final gem of neighbourhood trivia.

"Malmesbury is where the first person in Britain was killed by a tiger!"

This immediately piqued my interest. One of my dubious claims to fame is that I was once bitten by a tiger. And a lion. [1]

"Hannah Twynnoy was a barmaid in a local pub. In 1703, a travelling menagerie pitched up in the pub yard."

I had to suppress a giggle when Mike revealed the name of the tavern. "It was The White Lion..."

It seems Hannah wasn't an entirely innocent party in the tiger coming to tea. A plaque, now lost, recorded that despite 'repeated remonstrance from its keeper', she 'imprudently took pleasure' in tormenting the tiger. Of course, the day came when she enraged the beast so much, it broke free and turned her into the country's first human tiger tucker.

Who paid for Hannah's gravestone is an enduring mystery. It was unusual for any female – never mind a serving girl – to be given a lasting memorial. However, a stone in the Abbey grounds, engraved with a lyrical epitaph, still commemorates Hannah's passing:

In bloom of life
She's snatched from hence
She had no room
To make defence
For Tyger fierce
Took life away
And here she lies in a bed of clay
Until the Resurrection Day.

---

1. I would love to pretend that my big cat bites were a consequence of some heroic feat in an exotic corner of the globe, but it was a cub-cuddling session at a small zoo in rural Hertfordshire, England!

In contrast, the parish register sums up her demise with such dead-pan brevity it is almost funny:

"Hannah Twynney kild by a Tygre at ye White Lyon."

For me, this brought to mind Ogden Nash's poem, The Panther, which in six lines, offers sound advice on managing interactions with ferocious felines. Since it remains under copyright – and I don't want to fling a third genus into Malmesbury's minestrone of lily-toned lions and testy tigers – I have penned my own parody as a warning against messing with the stripey species:

If Malmesbury's tiger bares his fang,
You'll have no time to utter 'dang!'
And should the tiger proffer tea,
Decline with haste – and promptly flee!
For if you answer the tiger's call,
You likely won't come back at all...

Malmesbury has long been somewhere that people push their luck with the forces of nature. We know this because William of Malmesbury – the renowned medieval historian – recorded the exploits of his contemporary, Brother Eilmer, in his *Gesta Regum Anglorum (Deeds of English Kings)*.

William records how Eilmer prophesied the Norman invasion of England when he saw Halley's Comet in 1066. He quotes Eilmer as saying, "I see you brandishing the downfall of my country."

He goes on to describe William the Conqueror as a person of 'extraordinary corpulence', bald of brow, with a fierce countenance, and so strong that on horseback at full gallop, he could bend a bow that no one else could draw.

Yet, divining an event that would reshape English history wasn't Eilmer's most memorable feat.

The Abbey's great library placed Malmesbury among medieval Europe's foremost intellectual centres. Malmesbury's William described Eilmer as 'a man learned for those times.' It was doubtless here, among musty scrolls and weighty, leather-bound tomes, that Eilmer first read the Greek myth of Daedalus and his son, Icarus. Imprisoned in a tower by King Minos of Crete, Daedalus fashioned wings of feathers and wax to facilitate their escape. Daedalus warned Icarus to be bold, but not too bold – and not to fly too high.

But Icarus ignored his father's advice. Overcome with the joy of flight, Icarus flew too close to the sun. The heat melted his waxen wings, and he plummeted into the sea and drowned.

Inspired by airborne dreams, Eilmer decided to emulate Daedalus.

Sometime around the year 1000, he strapped makeshift wings to his hands and feet and enacted one of the earliest recorded attempts at human flight. Eilmer hurled himself from the Abbey tower and, miraculously, soared for 'more than a furlong' (660 ft or 200 m). He crash-landed and broke both legs – but earned both his wings and immortality. A millennium after his heroic attempt, we still remember Eilmer, 'The Flying Monk.'

"I forgot to provide myself a tail," he noted later, with casual understatement. Modern aerodynamic studies confirm that Eilmer's analysis of his failure was bang on – a tail would certainly have helped to stabilise his flight, but the Abbot forbade any further attempts to reach for the sky.

Despite being 'lame ever after', at least Eilmer survived to tell the tale, proving that in Malmesbury, curiosity doesn't always kill you – but the cat might.

***

These days, Malmesbury's White Lion pub is a private residence, and the George Inn is a veterinary practice. Make of that what you will, while we continue to chase our dreams like a tiger on the prowl.

Although the firing squad of fate was about to blow our plans apart.

Chapter 30

Broken Glass & Broken Plans: Bournemouth

"**G**o on. Give us a clue."

We'd spent a glamorous night on a Bournemouth industrial estate, outside Paranoid Plumbing, as I like to call the company that supplied our water heater. The boss – I want to call him Marvin (fans of *Hitchhiker's Guide to the Galaxy* will know why) – looked less than thrilled to be faced with a giant NATO-green pantechnicon parked on his forecourt on a Monday morning.

"We have an appointment," we explained. "Our water heater leaks, it pops every so often, and it won't work on mains power."

"You've picked the worst week," Marvin sighed. "I'm here on my own. If it's leaking, it will have to come out. And the popping sounds like a cracked igniter."

Our hearts sank.

But as he scrabbled about beneath our sink, his disembodied voice announced, "No wonder it's leaking. The pressure relief valve isn't connected to anything!"

Marvin reappeared and explained, "As the water heats, it expands and builds up pressure. So the boiler vents, and the water has to go somewhere. At the moment, it's just dripping out."

He drilled a hole in the floor, fitted a short length of plastic pipe to the valve, and hey presto. No more soggy carpet.

Marvin's second rummage beneath the sink exposed a further mystery.

"There's a switch under here that's turned off."

He turned on the switch and guess what...

It's fair to say our electrical setup, fitted by our friend Iain, was somewhat eccentric. We didn't suspect the water heater had an additional switch to activate mains power. Why would we? It was nowhere near any of the other switches, and buried in a completely inaccessible place at the back of the cupboard under the sink.

Next, Marvin peered at the heater's outside vent.

"Why have you put this grill over it?"

"To protect the vent."

"It's not necessary," Marvin said. "The holes in the grill act like a venturi. When it's windy, they suck out the air and extinguish the pilot light. When it relights, that's what's popping."

He removed the cover, and I can reveal our heater has never popped since.

Marvin stomped back indoors to prepare our bill, while Mark and I vowed never again to speak of this disgrace...

We thought our humiliation was complete until we met Tom, Marvin's next client, who had pulled up next to us in his van.

He invited himself in for a nose around The Beast and, as a bonus, shed light upon another enigma – our solar controller.

For months, we'd noted down the readings, trying to make sense of how they related to our batteries' state of charge.

"The bars on the battery icon change all the time," we told him.

"Yes," Tom replied. "They would, because they're just a snapshot of what's coming in at that moment."

Like storm clouds parting, he'd revealed the reason our painstakingly recorded data made no sense. All this time, we'd simply maintained a diligent log of random numbers!

"We've also noticed the PV reading just keeps going up," we told him.

"Of course." Tom grinned. "That's just telling you your total usage since you installed the system."

***

We had returned to base since our van, Big Blue's MOT was due. Plus, we wanted to take advantage of the autumn gales to score a bit of windsurfing.

After spending the rest of the day checking every bulb and brake light, we took Big Blue for her test. She passed with flying colours, so we repaired to a tranquil spot in the New Forest to reward ourselves with an early evening nap.

As I dozed, Mark seemed obsessed with peering out of the rear blinds. As dusk fell, he refused to let me take the dogs out.

"A car just stopped behind us, flashed its lights five times, then drove off," he hissed.

I opened one eye and mumbled, "What?"

"Shhhh. Now, there's a woman dressed entirely in black walking down the road."

His continued curtain-twitching exposed a shock revelation.

"She's picked up a carrier bag from behind that gatepost!"

That woke me up. I crept to the slit in the blinds, and we both watched as she slid into a car, executed a U-turn with her headlights off, and vanished into the darkness.

"I think we've just witnessed a drug deal..." Mark said.

Suddenly, our 'tranquil spot' seemed a little less inviting. We waited a while to ensure that while we were watching them, no one had been watching us, then upped and moved to the lay-by where we started our travels, all those months before.

Despite our flight from the underworld goings-on, we still had a disturbed night. Gales rocked and rattled The Beast all night. The following morning, battered and bleary-eyed, we took the dogs out and couldn't believe what we saw.

"Do you think it was a stone that flew up from a passing car?" I asked Mark. "Or something blown around by the wind?"

"No. You can see the impact point here," he said. "It looks like we've been shot!"

Right on the edge of our windscreen, a cobweb of cracked glass radiated out from a single, small, circular bullseye.

A fresh wave of despair engulfed me.

One shattered windscreen had been enough. A second felt like a curse, but this was not the last piece of bad news the day had in store.

Chapter 31

Mercy Dash

"**B**ut what about your family and friends?" is a popular square on our imaginary Lorry Life Bingo card.

The conversation usually goes along the lines of: "We'd LOVE to retire early and hit the road like you!" Then in almost the same breath, they add: "Of course, we couldn't leave the kids / grandkids / our elderly parents…"

We understand.

The pull of family is real, and the guilt can be heavy, but to live life, especially outside society's norms, there are tough decisions to make.

That said, we're aware that sometimes, people reach for family as an excuse.

We've heard every version from, "The grandkids would never forgive us!" to "I'd do it like a shot – but the wife / 'im indoors would never go for it."

We know perfectly well what they are saying.

They will never go for it.

They have never intended to go for it.

They are simply not being honest about the reasons.

My mum and Mark's dad had already passed away when we set

out on our extended tours. This added a crescendo to the chorus of opinions about whether it was 'right' to leave behind an elderly widow and widower to travel for months at a time.

We were certain our parents had the care and company they needed, but still the judgement poured in.

The truth is, there's no one-size-fits-all solution. Everyone's circumstances are different, and the decisions you make must reflect that. However, the point will always come where you need to balance duty with the reality that life is short.

Redundancy provided the push, but as I mentioned previously, the shocking loss of several friends – two of whom were younger than us – was also a major factor in our decision to fulfil our dreams of travel. It was a wake-up call. The one that forced home the realisation: waiting for the 'right time' was a gamble.

Because the 'right time' may never come.

Our first philosophy is that *you must live life.*

We don't have kids, but if we did, they would still have their futures ahead of them. Our parents have lived their lives how they chose. While it is essential to be compassionate and look after those dearest to us, our own needs and desires matter too.

Our second philosophy is: *what's right for you is right for the world.* It might sound selfish, but living purely to please everyone else, or meet others' expectations breeds resentment. That is not right for you or the world – and particularly not right for the people it causes you to resent.

As we pursued our careers, family considerations led us to shelve some of our dreams and ambitions. We turned down opportunities to live and work abroad when we saw the reaction it provoked in our parents. We hold no grudges, because although we took their wishes into account, the decision not to go was entirely ours. But now in our late 50s, time and options could be running out. We are fortunate that when opportunity knocked, we were still fit and healthy enough to do what we love. We can windsurf, hike, and ski at an advanced level – and want to make the most of it while we can.

And then there is our third philosophy. The one forged in the fire of Building The Beast: *there's always a solution...*

We balance our lifestyle and responsibilities by returning to the UK regularly to spend quality time with our nearest and dearest. While we are away, we keep in regular touch. We are available 24-hours a day on the other end of a mobile phone, and I am probably one of the few people on Earth who still send postcards. Appearing on the doormat like a smile amid the junk and bills, they tell the recipient they're truly in your thoughts.

These days, the internet allows us to have essentials such as groceries delivered – we even arranged a replacement fridge for Mark's mum remotely. We're never more than a few hours' flight away. So, should a serious problem arise, we can be back in the UK faster than you could say, "abdication of responsibility."

The 'few-hours'-flight-rule' also works the other way. Friends and relatives can – and do – come out to meet up on our travels, so we're not entirely cut off.

You might say this all sounds good in theory – but we have put it into practice. The 'family question' caught up with us one December, when both Mark's mum and his brother vanished at the same time. They share a home, so it took several frantic calls before we discovered they'd both been admitted to hospital on the same day, entirely independently, and for unrelated reasons.

Faster than you could shout, "dereliction of duty", Mark was on a plane from Italy back to Blighty, while I spent Christmas and New Year on my own, up a mountain in a blizzard, caring for five dogs. (The

Fifth Man was a stray we adopted in Romania).

When Mark returned to Italy in January, our ski season ended. We packed up our caravan and drove home to look after them both.

If we're needed, we will always be there.

Although it is invariably a shock, at nearly 96, Mark's mum going into hospital was not completely unexpected. The real bombshell was his brother. Outwardly fit and healthy, he collapsed in the street, was rushed to hospital, and diagnosed with a rare and aggressive form of cancer. His prognosis for survival was next to nil.

Seven years on, I am delighted to say he defied medical science and is fully in remission, but the moral of this story is that if you really want to travel, there will be a solution: a way to accommodate your loved ones' needs. It's merely a question of finding a balance.

Of course, it is up to each individual to identify their priorities, and confront the inevitable disapproval. Because whatever you choose, there is always someone waiting in the wings, poised and ready to criticise.

However, if ever there was a lesson in living your life to the full because you can't predict what's around the corner, the story of Mark's brother is it.

***

Which brings me to a storm that had been brewing for a while.

I phoned my dad, and something in his voice set off alarms. He sounded very odd and distant.

I had not seen him for two years. Although we spoke on the phone every Sunday, Dad had barred everyone from visiting, including me and all remaining family. When COVID struck, he couldn't have been happier. A deadly virus was the perfect justification to keep people away.

Dad is my hero. He is a quiet, intelligent person who enjoys his own company. Never one for socialising or snack conversation, at 86, he is still happiest watching the cricket, or applying himself to the Guardian cryptic crossword – a puzzle so devious I can't even work it out if he gives me the answers. When I call, a two-minute chat hits record-breaking territory for length.

He is a proud man, so I had some suspicions about his motives for refusing visitors. Sadly, my worst fears turned out to be true. He'd retreated to conceal a multitude of age-related problems, all of which were getting worse. And now, it seemed, an entire flock of chickens had suddenly come home to roost.

My brother told me Dad's neighbour, Denise, had called him. Denise kept an eye on Dad, and nipped in daily to make sure he was okay.

Dad clearly felt Denise's kind heart was the perfect solution – enough to get by, while shielding him from family nagging to take care of himself. But as he deteriorated, poor Denise reached her wit's end. She was already caring for her own parents and a disabled sibling; adding my increasingly needy dad was a step too far. Obviously, we were unaware of quite how bad things had got, because Dad had kept us all at arm's length.

"I think something happened around the 11th of October," my brother said. "Dad had a stroke or a fall – he won't say – but he's lost his sight."

As we did two years previously for Mark's family, we dropped everything to answer the call of caring duties, and set course for Lancashire.

Mark and I drove up separately – I went on ahead in our newly

MOT'd van, Big Blue. Even if Dad could clamber up three steps into The Beast's cab, it was not a vehicle that would cut it for running errands or attending medical appointments. We needed The Beast to live in because my dad has an almost pathological fear of dogs, so although he had three spare bedrooms, with our furry family, we could not stay with him.

***

Blackburn in Lancashire is an old cotton-milling town in the north-west of England. It is not somewhere people choose to go on holiday, so it is not replete with accommodation. We knew of a five-van camp-site near my dad's: we'd stayed there with the caravan, so we had every confidence The Beast would not fit through the gate!

While immunosuppressed from chemotherapy, Mark's brother could not have contact with The Pawsome Foursome. While we cared for him, we maintained separation by spending the summer rather bizarrely living in our caravan, parked on the front lawn of his mum's suburban Surrey bungalow. This was not an option with Dad. He lives on a main road, and The Beast is far too huge to fit on his drive, which also slopes at the sort of angle that would require ropes and crampons for us to climb into bed.

With a top speed of 45 mph, The Beast performed a stately 300-mile mercy dash.

At the helm of Big Blue, I was much quicker, so I drove straight to Dad's.

I rang the bell and called, "It's Jackie!" as I let myself in with my key.

"Oh, my lovely daughter," Dad replied.

Despite everything, he was in good spirits.

I think he was relieved that the subterfuge was over and the cavalry had arrived, but it shocked me to see how frail he'd become. In his prime, my dad was over six feet tall with a shock of flame-red curls. He was a maths teacher and a mountaineer. Never mind fairy tales, as a child, he captivated me with Einstein's theories of relativity and the Apollo moon landings. He introduced me to the wit of writers and poets such as Patrick Campbell, Ogden Nash, and Tom Lehrer, and we regularly wrote each other silly poems. Since I could toddle, we'd hiked together. I know he ignited a spark in me – and many of his pupils – that led to a lifelong love of the outdoors. Yet what greeted me as I entered the lounge was a bent, white-haired old man, sitting crookedly in a chair, whose sightless eyes were almost popping out of his head.

Dad has always been squeamish about eyes. The mere thought of my contact lenses made him squirm. His sisters all had cataract operations, but he couldn't countenance the idea, so he dealt with his fading sight as he did with most issues – he pretended it wasn't happening. He hadn't seen an optician for over 20 years. When we finally got an ophthalmologist to come to the house, he diagnosed advanced cataracts and glaucoma – an increase in pressure in the eye. No wonder Dad's eyes were bulging like Popeye's.

I hugged Dad and sat down.

"I'm sorry, but I just can't have the dogs here," he blurted.

"I know," I replied gently. "And I wouldn't ask you to. We'll stay in The Beast and Mark can look after the unmentionables."

Dad smiled. 'Unmentionables' was a jocular conversational accommodation we'd arrived at to reference The Fab Four.

Despite his blindness, Dad was coping remarkably well. He'd got used to covering up his problems – he remembered where he kept everything and navigated by counting strides between items of furniture. His sudden loss of sight meant he struggled to prepare meals and hot drinks, which is where Denise had kindly stepped in. He was no cook. For years, he'd lived on a diet of bananas, mini pork pies, and sandwiches, and didn't mind a cup of cold coffee. So, Denise could leave him some filled rolls and a few mugs of coffee, and he was sorted for the day.

I explained to Dad that Denise is a wonderful person, but relying on her selfless generosity was not fair or sustainable.

"I don't want to go in a home!"

I grasped his hand in both of mine to assuage his angst.

"None of us want that," I said, "and it doesn't need to happen if we can get a few things in place to help you stay at home."

Dad had lived in the same house since 1961. I was born in the front bedroom, and Denise's parents were already living next door when Mum and Dad moved in. He had long-standing ties to those bricks and mortar.

Two hours later, Mark called me from a local pub.

"They do Park4Night here. I've met Pete, the landlord, and he was really understanding. I told him what had happened, and he said, 'I've just lost my mum, so I know exactly how you feel. Stay as long as you like.'"

At least that was our first problem solved – we had somewhere to live.

I'm not sure Pete reckoned on us still being there three months later, but without his open-hearted generosity, I have no idea what we would have done.

Chapter 32

Oh My Cron!

I have nothing but admiration for carers, who often surrender their entire existence to look after others. Certainly, my first few weeks in Lancashire gave me an excellent taste of what full-time personal care involved.

Four times a day, I drove fifteen minutes each way from the pub to Dad's. I got him up, made his breakfast, lunch, and dinner, then settled him to bed. On top of that came housework, shopping, walking the dogs, modifying the house to suit his needs, and setting up outside care. There was a family tightrope to navigate. Mark and I had already done all this for his mum, so we knew what was required and how to go about it, but as the eldest, my brother preferred to take the lead. When he visited from London, we'd endure countless meetings with agencies and occupational health, trying to get a support package in place. I was happy to step back, because fortunately, we were on the same page about our objective: to do everything we could to keep Dad at home.

In the meantime, I held the fort, camped on a soggy Lancashire pub car park like a bedraggled version of Alan Bennett's *Lady in the Van*.

Once we established a system of carers coming in three times a day, it relieved some of the daily pressure on me. Even so, the next few months involved endless rounds of medical appointments – getting Dad vaccinated against flu and COVID, taking him to eye clinics and the doctor to address a multitude of issues he'd ignored. My goal was to get Dad comfortable with the carers, and into a position to remain sustainably in his own home without me or my brother in attendance full-time.

Before we could consider cataract surgery, we needed to bring the glaucoma under control with drops – which Dad loathed – to see if there was any hope of restoring some vision.

Dad's confidence crumbled when he lost his sight. The consequent lack of exercise meant he was weak, and ever more prone to the risk of a fall. My brother organised weekly physiotherapy home visits to rebuild Dad's strength. I attended them all for moral support and did my best to encourage the reluctant subject to persevere with the recommended exercises in between.

As far as the house went, Dad refused everything we suggested – chair raisers, walking aids – the lot. We tried to reason with him, pointing out that these gadgets might make his life easier and, more importantly, keep him in his beloved home. At times, I could have screamed with exasperation, but I understood. Accepting help meant accepting decline, and every concession was like handing over another slice of independence. For Dad, that was harder to stomach than the risk itself.

When we finally persuaded him to give it a try, we had to go through the entire set-up process again, because the initial assessments had expired. After many more meetings, he eventually conceded to having – and using – a stair rail. But the downstairs loo? Absolutely not. That would be surrender.

I pleaded with him.

"If you fall down the stairs, it's game over – and all our efforts will be in vain!"

But no amount of begging would persuade him.

Yet, for all the agonising frustration, I admired his bloody-mindedness. I am his daughter – a terrible patient – and have no doubt I would feel the same.

I left Mark to sort out The Beast's broken windscreen. At least this time, we knew it was a simple fix, but it was another problem to solve in a season already overflowing with obstacles. I scarcely had a moment to think about myself, but realising we'd be grounded for a few months, I applied for my provisional lorry licence.

I always encourage fellow females to hone the skills to drive their own leisure vehicles. First, it's definitely worth it for the looks you get as a woman in charge of a large vehicle. Second, there's no reason why you can't do it – it's not a feat of physical prowess. But third, and most importantly, if your designated driver is ill or has even a minor accident, you're stuck. Had I been unable to take the wheel and tow our caravan, we would have spent weeks stranded in Budapest because Mark cracked his ribs and couldn't drive.

I still relish the sight of the burger seller who spotted me exiting the campsite in Hungary. He hid behind his food cart, clearly terrified that I was about to mow him down and plough my 40 ft (12 m) rig through his epicurean empire. All because of ovaries!

Lancashire is on the windward side of the Pennines, which is what made its climate perfect for cotton milling and weaving. The all-pervading damp stopped the threads from breaking.

"Since we arrived in Lancashire, we've had four dry days!" I told my friend, Elaine, on the phone. "With four soggy doggies, the truck is awash with mud and condensation. The only change is whether the rain lashes in sideways from the left, or the right!"

It was a miserable existence, and as the days shortened, we watched our solar system gradually lose the will to live. I pined for the blue skies and snow-covered pistes of Italy.

Mark made an appointment with a local campervan electrical specialist. When he arrived on site with The Beast, the foreman took one look at Iain's wild jungle of wires and issued a swift diagnosis.

"I'm not touchin' that, mate!"

Luckily, Peter, a chap I'd met on social media, dropped by for a pint and demystified some of our solar sorrows.

I was only just getting my head around solar technology, having previously categorised it as a close cousin of alchemy, witchcraft, and voodoo.

"The fridge needs 12 volts to work," Peter said. "As the batteries discharge, the voltage drops. If it goes below 12 volts, the fridge will cut out. But as the fridge warms up inside, its thermostat tries to restart the compressor, which demands power. Then, it gets into a vicious cycle – demanding power and draining power – which discharges the batteries even further."

With 1300 watts of solar and 720 amp hours of battery, everyone, including the guys who fitted it, had high expectations of our electrical setup. But a northwest December was not producing enough power to keep us going. On the rare occasions when the sun emerged, the solar panels were generating only 4 amps. When it was overcast – which it was most of the time – we harvested a measly 0.4 amps of sunshine. And outside the hours of 10 a.m. and 2 p.m., the sun disappeared behind the pub roof.

"In winter, besides the short days, the sun is low in the sky," Peter told us. "So the panels are probably only working at 20% efficiency. If you could angle them towards the sun, that would improve – that's why you often see tilting solar panels on canal boats."

Peter also shed light on another electrical issue regarding our AGM (Absorbent Glass Mat) gel batteries. We chose AGM because the technology is well established and robust, but we had failed to grasp one huge detail.

"You can only discharge AGM batteries to 50% without damaging them. So, although nominally you have 720 amp hours of power, only 360 amp hours of that is usable. In theory, lithium batteries can discharge fully. It may shorten their life, but with lithium, it's almost all usable power."

Peter continued, "At 50%, your battery bank stores around 4 kilowatts of power. The fridge probably uses 1 kilowatt per day."

It was a lightbulb moment.

Mark and I looked at each other with new understanding.

Even 4 amps represented an incoming charge of only 0.05 kilowatts.

No wonder our electrical system was slowly dying.

***

Dad's carers seemed to be working out, and we were going all out to help him become self-sufficient. Yet as we moved into winter, coronavirus cases were rising, so we were not sure the EU would welcome British citizens. Nevertheless, we still clung to the hope we'd be able to grab some precious time on the slopes before the season ended.

However, the fates had different plans.

Although less severe, a new, more contagious and vaccine-resistant Omicron coronavirus variant emerged in the UK, resulting in rapid and extensive outbreaks.

On 17th December 2021, due to the surge in cases, France announced a ban on British travellers entering the country. The Netherlands was already in lockdown, and Germany teetering on the brink.

Our friends Stuart and Charlotte, the Orkney Overlanders, got out of Britain just in time and set off to tour Spain.

But, once again, border closures trapped us on our home turf.

Not that I could travel in any case – because I had ceased to exist.

My passport was with the Italian embassy, seeking a long-stay visa, and my driving licence was pursuing a truck licence with the DVLA. With no formal identification, I was a nonperson!

Which posed a further conundrum.

All our ski gear – thousands of pounds' worth of skis, avalanche safety equipment, and winter clothing – was enjoying a long sabbatical in Italy without us. When we escaped our Italian lockdown in June, we'd left it stashed in the ski locker of the apartment we rent for the season. After all, we were *certain* we'd be back in a few months. But now, we couldn't get there to collect it – and the thought of the place being re-let with our gear in the way, or worse, going walkabout, made us sweat like beginners on a black run.

As we're fond of saying, there's always a solution, so we posted a locker key to our friends Carlos and Ezio in the ski shop. They kindly recovered our gear and promised to keep it safe until we could return to Italy to collect it.

Then, just before Christmas, we got the news that Italy refused to have us.

It might surprise you to learn we were not sorry.

Although the visa seemed like a Brexit panacea because it would allow us unlimited time in Italy, while still keeping our 90 days in Schengen – there is inevitably a fly in the ointment.

That fly appeared in the guise of an unexpected tax that, until recently, had evaded our radar of fastidious research.

We were aware that, like most countries, Italy has a dual tax agreement with the UK. This means you can't be taxed for the same thing in both countries. The fly was the sudden discovery that, in addition to the reciprocal arrangement, Italy operates a wealth tax on overseas property and pensions. This is to prevent its citizens from pursuing the popular Italian pastime of tax evasion, by offshoring their assets to avoid paying their dues.

Unfortunately for us, it meant we faced losing 1/3 of our earnings from our not-so-vast real estate rental empire and paltry pensions. Since we can't survive on 2/3 of our income, Italian residency was a non-starter!

***

We enjoyed a lovely family Christmas with Dad. My brother and his girlfriend came, and it was a jovial occasion. Although everything was different, it was almost like old times.

But the world was on edge.

As the anniversary of the storming of the US Capitol passed on 6th January – commemorating a murderous mob of Trump supporters attempting to overturn the result of a democratic election – news came in that Russian tanks were rolling into Kazakhstan to crush protests about soaring fuel prices. There was unrest in Armenia, and the Azerbaijan land border remained closed because of pandemic restrictions.

Mass uprisings, border closures, violent crackdowns, and curfews dogged our route to Mongolia.

On 14th January 2022, France opened its borders to vaccinated Brits, but we couldn't travel because we still needed to care for Dad.

We had arranged a consultation with an eye specialist in February, after which he might need two separate cataract operations. Reluctantly, we shelved our skiing ambitions and accepted another ski season lost.

Then on 24th February came the shock news that Russian president Vladimir Putin had launched a full-scale invasion of Ukraine – the largest attack on a European country since World War II.

Forces entered Ukraine from Russia, Belarus, and Crimea, which Russia annexed in 2014.

Beyond the horror, it marked the end of our dream.

With war raging across the region, the road east to Mongolia – the one we built The Beast to follow – had been devoured by chaos.

Chapter 33

Epilogue

We'd had coronavirus, Brexit, and our replacement-for-Mongolia tour had turned into a game of Scottish snakes and ladders. Every foray north had been thwarted by some devious serpent, which had sent us sliding straight back to base on the south coast.

In the end, we felt like we'd undergone a vehicular Labour of Hercules – although when your vehicle is also your home, the stakes are considerably higher than mere immortality.

But we'd tamed The Beast: survived Trial by Trilex, two broken windscreens, and sourced impossible-to-find parts. We'd wrestled with an electrical setup that resembled an avant-garde art installation, a popping propane heater, and knew which nipples to grease and – maybe – when. We'd got a 'Go-Anywhere' truck stuck, rescued ourselves, and could reel off Lorry Life Bingo answers in our sleep.

As we awaited Dad's optical assessment, we went south once again, and Luke's Vanlife fitted the critical battery monitor and battery-to-battery charger. At last, the blinkers were lifted. We could check our batteries' state of charge at will, and top them up as we drove.

When Luke showed us his own immaculate power system, it sowed the seed for a long-term solution to our electrical afflictions.

"I made a feature of it," he said. "It's all Victron. The components are available worldwide, and they all talk to each other. You can track everything from your smartphone – and support can access it remotely for troubleshooting."

Mounted neatly on a backing of gleaming stainless steel chequer plate, the whole futuristic installation flashed and shone like the bridge of the Starship Enterprise.

And I wanted it.

Through a lack of understanding and knowledge, our solar setup was the epitome of that classic mistake: buy cheap, buy twice. In anticipation of far flung adventures, it made sense to replace the beating heart of The Beast with a decent, reliable system which came with global support.

By the end of our unexpected British tour, we knew far more than when we started. Talk about 'fake it 'til you make it'.

On reflection, we were relieved that we'd tested The Beast in Britain instead of launching ourselves headlong towards Central Asia. We'd got used to her quirks, determined her limitations, and solved the never-ending list of snags in a place where we could at least speak the language and get help. Even if it had sometimes taken months to find out where.

Through devious meanderings, we had truly discovered beauty in our backyard. Our random routes uncovered so much that is overlooked: lost kings, vanished capitals, and a village with a population of 35 that could have changed the course of British history. Plus, along the way, we'd found our tribe.

Not just fellow nomads and lorry lifers who completely understood our burning compulsion to travel, but a home-away-from-home at a Lancashire pub. It was the first time since I left at seventeen that I'd stayed in my hometown for longer than a fleeting visit, and I experienced a strong sense of belonging.

I'd spent my entire adult life as a misfit in the South of England, mocked for my funny accent and wild eccentricities, such as a natural urge to chat to anyone who happened to be next to me – tantamount to declaring yourself an axe murderer on the London Underground! Yet here, everyone sounded the same as me. They were open, sociable, and didn't think I was a raving alcoholic if I said I fancied a 'brew' at ten o'clock in the morning.

I had reconnected with my roots, and confirmed that 'home' isn't a point on a map. It's a feeling that finds you when you stop searching. A quiet contentment that grows where connection, love, laughter – and shared journeys intertwine.

Society is always chasing the future, and most people put themselves in voluntary slavery to get there. We'd found an alternative: a way to live with less, and fully in the present. But we had also learned that whatever path you choose, there is no escaping problems. There is no stress-free lifestyle; no perfect adventure. Outside factors – breakdowns, bureaucracy, and the tug of love – had dictated our entire route. True freedom remained an illusion, tantalisingly unattainable.

But every setback taught us something vital: it's not what happens, but how you deal with it that counts. That cup of tea – taking a moment to assess and make a plan – can be the difference between success and failure. And as generations of self-improvement gurus have said, *Happiness is not getting what you want, it's wanting what you get.*

And through it all, the dogs reminded us what really matters. Their joy was pure and uncomplicated. Their tails still wagged in the rain as they buried their noses in fresh scents – thrilled just to be together. When life pelted us with detours and setbacks, they didn't care about maps or miles, only that the pack was together for the ride. If there was ever a masterclass on living in the moment, it came with fur and four paws.

We never made it to Scotland, Mongolia, or half the places we'd planned – but we'd lived the dream on a few soggy car parks, lay-bys, industrial estates – and countless magical locations that most tourists will never see.

And although Scotland eluded us, we'd achieved the next best thing – we'd been to Corby, 'the Glasgow of the South'!

Life rarely unfolds as expected, but that's the allure. The journey itself is the point. Invariably, there are diversions, mishaps, and unforeseen hurdles. But there's also laughter, camaraderie, and joy that give you the courage to keep moving forward. Plus, the thrill of discovering that sometimes, the muddy, messy, brilliant road you end up on is way more rewarding than the one you had envisioned.

Unfortunately, when we eventually saw the eye specialist, he diagnosed that Dad's advanced glaucoma had caused too much damage to rescue his sight. However, with the help of carers, Dad reached a level of self-sufficiency that allowed us to breathe without constant guilt. Finally, we could look to our own future.

With Mongolia out of reach, we needed a new plan.

Somewhere wild, somewhere different.

We thought about a country that until recently had been completely closed to outsiders. It was rich in history, had stunning landscapes and beaches, and, crucially, was outside Schengen.

Mark grinned and laid out a tempting option for our next trip.

"Never mind the Balkans. What about Albania?"

Author's Note
- Imperial vs
Metric

I am a child of the '60s, brought up with feet, inches, and yards. We had pints of milk, and 240 pennies in a pound. I still understand weight in pounds, ounces, and stones, although a tonne is roughly a ton (and even they differ in the US and UK) so I've stuck with that. As for distance, I can only appreciate that in feet, inches, yards, or miles. We get hot weather a bit more frequently these days, but for me, it still needs to come in Fahrenheit.

I was living in an imperial world, and I am an imperial girl!

Britain committed to the metric system in 1965, but not whole-heartedly. We kept things like pints and miles. As a scientist, I got used to expressing volumes in litres (although I know a pint is about 500 ml) and find it easier to understand cold temperatures in Celsius. After all, 0°C is far more straightforward than 32°F, and -10 sounds bloody cold. 30°C means nothing to me, but if you tell me the temperature is in the mid-eighties, you will find me sprinting into the shade.

I still can't visualise the height of a mountain unless I multiply by three to convert metres roughly into feet. As for kilometres – I just divide by two and hope for the best.

Then we bought a European truck, whose dimensions are all in metres, and travel in Europe, where they started doing everything in metric in the 1700s.

So, dear reader, throughout the text, I have attempted to convert imperial to metric for your convenience. I have tried to be systematic about it, but please understand that I have a split personality and sometimes just revert to the hard yards (which equate to approximately a metre!)

Thank You!

Thank you so much for reading my story. The Fab Four, Mark, and I hope you enjoyed it.

If you have a moment, we would be unbelievably grateful if you could leave a review on Amazon, Goodreads, BookBub – or anywhere else – to tell others what you thought of the book.

It can be as short as you like.

I read all the reviews, so if you learned something, felt inspired, had a giggle at our misfortunes, or anything else, a single sentence will make my day. Not only that, honest reviews help readers to find my books. As an independent author, I don't have the marketing might of a publishing company behind me, so your reviews and ratings really matter.

And if you could tell your friends or share it on social media, I will love you even more.

If you want to be the first to know when I release a new book, here are a few ways to keep in touch:

- Author Website

  - https://jacquelinelambert.co.uk

- Travel Blog:

  - https://www.WorldWideWalkies.com

- Facebook:

  - https://www.facebook.com/JacquelineLambertAuthor

- Amazon:

  - https://www.amazon.com/author/jacquelinelambert

- Goodreads:

  - https://www.goodreads.com/author/show/18672478.J acqueline_Lambert

- Bookbub:

  - https://www.bookbub.com/profile/jacqueline-lambert

Besides stories and photos from our travels, my blog has tips and printable checklists for travel with dogs, details of how we fund our lifestyle, and links to suppliers we used in the construction of The Beast.

I am also a member of We Love Memoirs, the friendliest group on Facebook.

WLM connects readers and authors to discuss all kinds of memoirs, including travellers' 'tails' like this one.

If memoirs, competitions, or book giveaways are your thing, pop in and say 'Hi' there too!

Thank you!

By The Same Author

Adventure Caravanning with Dogs Series

Year 1 – Fur Babies in France – From Wage Slaves to Living the Dream

The true story of a couple who accidentally bought their first caravan – then decided to give up work, rent out the house, and tour Europe full-time with their four dogs. This book follows their first year on wheels, which involved lots of breakages, following a near-death experience on Day 1...

> *"Full of fun. Told with excitement, vibrancy, and humour." Julie Haigh, Goodreads Librarian and Top 1,000 Amazon Reviewer*

"Well written, full of bounce and fun." Valerie Poore,
Author and blogger at Marvellous Memoirs: Reviews
and links

Dog on the Rhine – From Rat Race to Road Trip

Now, with a little caravanning experience under their belts, the crew get a bit more adventurous and cross Germany, before going on a brief bark around the Balkans (the Czech Republic, Slovenia and Croatia). But lest they mislead you into thinking that Livin' the Dream is all sunshine and rainbows, they return home to a huge Fidose of reality...

> *"An inspirational travelogue." Windyoneuk on Ama zon.co.uk*

> *"Makes me want to take my dog, buy a caravan, and go traveling." Chris on Goodreads*

Dogs 'n' Dracula – A Road Trip Through Romania

WINNNER: Chill With A Book Premier Readers'
Award, 2022

FINALIST: Romania Insider Awards for Best Pro-
motion of Romania Abroad, 2019

Told they would be robbed, scammed, kidnapped by gypsies, eaten
by bears or attacked by wild dogs and wolves, if they managed to
avoid the floods, riots – and vampires – the team Boldly Go Where
No Van Has Gone Before. Join them as they explore Europe's largest
wilderness, adopt a street dog, and tow a caravan across the Carpathian
Mountains on one of the world's most dangerous roads.

*"Armchair travel delight." Frances Hampson on Ama
zon.com*

*"A delightful book about the nomad lifestyle." Sharon
Geitz, Gum Trees and Galaxies*

It Never Rains But It Paws – A Road Trip Through Politics And A Pandemic

Five years after giving up work to travel full-time, Jackie and Mark race against time to leave the UK before Britain exits the EU. If Brexit happens, their four precious pups will lose their pet passports and will be unable to travel. But Brexit isn't their only obstacle. How do they cope when, a few months into their trip, the pandemic leaves them trapped in the epicentre of Europe's No.1 coronavirus hotspot?

> *"Her nimble writing rivals Bill Bryson and Paul Theroux." Liisa W. on Amazon.com*

> *"A very light-hearted and enjoyable read." Alison Williams (author), Alison Williams Writing*

To Hel in a Hound Cart – Journey To The Centre Of Europe

"Go to Hel!" The local wasn't being rude. She was describing Poland's best beach and windsurfing destination. Released from coronavirus lockdown, Jackie and Mark packed themselves and four dogs into their hound cart (RV), but are unsure where their wanderlust might take them. Their adventures soon start stacking up. Dodging precipitous cliff-side roads, political unrest, and a global pandemic, will they make it to Hel in a Hound Cart, or is that what will happen to their plans?

> *"Exuberant, sparkling with wit, insights, and well-researched historical facts... it's laugh-out-loud, poignant, and superbly written." Fi Kidd, Overland Adventurer*

> *"Her irrepressible sense of irreverent humour and quest for knowledge once more shine through." Sue Bavey, Author of Lucky Jack (1894-2000)*

Although part of a series which is chronological in time, and follows the author since giving up work to travel, each book is a stand-alone adventure.

Pups on Piste – A Ski Season in Italy

Jackie, Mark, and their canine crew spend three months in Monte Rosa, a little-known ski resort tucked under the second highest peak in Western Europe. It also happens to be in the world's Top 5 off-piste ski destinations. With parables from on piste and off, our snowmads get lost, stranded – and are told by an instructor, "Don't miss the turn or you'll go over a cliff."

> *"Highly recommended for dog lovers, ski enthusiasts, and adventure travellers." Louise Capper, Waggy Tales Book & Dog Blog.*

> *"Excellent reference book! Jackie's story telling and informative approach has not only relieved me of some of my anxieties (about a planned trip) but really inspired me! Most interesting is that it's a thoroughly good read by a very eloquent writer." Hannah James – Winteri sed.com Motorhome Skiing*

The Wayward Truck Series

Building The Beast – How (Not) To Build An Overland Camper

WINNER: The Wishing Shelf BRONZE Book Award 2024 – Adult Non-Fiction

WINNER: Readers' Favorite 5* Seal

FINALIST: Page Turner Book Awards 2024

The comic memoir of a crazy idea, *Building The Beast* chronicles Jackie and Mark's misadventures when they buy a 24.5-tonne army truck blind off the internet on Friday 13th, then attempt their first ever DIY campervan conversion. Their intention is to create an off-grid tiny home-on-wheels fit to undertake an overland expedition to Mongolia.

> *"For readers who love interesting characters interspersed with the practicalities of a nomadic lifestyle and the challenges of life on the road (or trying to get there), this book is a gem."* Reedsy Discovery

"This book is a fantastic look at designing a unique project and going for it with humor and perseverance. If one is tired of another 'chucking it all in and renovating an old house' story, this is a quixotic twist that will keep you entertained." Kari Iverson Lane

More Manchester Than Mongolia: An Unexpected Road Trip Through Back Road Britain

When COVID-19 derails their dream trip to Mongolia, Jackie, Mark, and their four dogs find themselves stranded in Blighty, in an army truck camper laughably over-engineered for the British countryside. Undeterred, they set out to explore the hidden marvels of their homeland, and discover whether fortune really does favour the brave.

"I haven't laughed so much at the written word since Pam Ayres released Some of Me Poetry *in 1976! Jacqueline Lambert has developed a style of writing comedic prose that is better than most comedy travel authors."* Drew Johnson, Author of the *Anadalucian Adventures* series

"Not so much a road trip round Britain, more a 'How DID we do that? WHY did we go up there? Well – we know not to do THAT again!' trip around Britain. Every chapter, another adventure or near disaster, told in Jackie's endearing and humorous fashion." Chris Moore, Beta Reader

Forthcoming books will follow the adventures of The Beast, their wayward truck, as it finally embarks on a foray east...

Anthologies

Travel Stories Series & Box Set, Curated by Alyson Sheldrake

Itchy Feet: Tales of travel and adventure

Come with us as we take an epic journey out of Africa, through the Indonesian jungle and raft the Zambezi. Ride a Harley through France and Spain and find out what makes someone a perpetual nomad. Itchy Feet was released to a string of five-star reviews. A free photo album accompanies each book in the Travel Stories series.

> *"An excellent choice for lovers of travel and adventure stories. It's one to dip in and out of or immerse oneself in. Either way, it's a thoroughly entertaining read." Beth Haslam, Vine Voice Reviewer and Author of the Fat Dogs and French Estates series*

Wish You Were Here: Holiday Memories

Whether it is a childhood 'bucket and spade' family holiday, the 'once-in-a-lifetime' dream destination, your first trip abroad, or the city where you first fell in love, we all have that one holiday that stands out in our minds. The award-winning and top travel memoir authors in this anthology bring out their postcards and photo albums and invite you to join them as they reminisce about their travels. Maybe they will inspire you to book your next holiday too!

> *"From Paris to Galapagos – from the comfort of our armchair – you'll wish you were there too." Jules Brown, Author of the Born to Travel Series: Tales from a Travel Writer's Life.*

The Travel Stories Box Set

With 17 (yes – *seventeen*) bonus chapters, including *A Honeymoon Horror Story* by yours truly, that's nearly a whole extra book!

Robert Fear Anthologies

40 Life Changing Events, 2022 edition

25 writers share events that have changed their lives. Some of these stories are tragic, others full of joy, but they all encapsulate tenacity, resilience, and self-belief. This fascinating compilation will encourage you to pause and reflect, with tales that offer much needed motivation and inspiration in these challenging times.

> *"From a letter to a past lover to the Namibian desert, dogs and thieves, there is a wealth of experiences to enjoy." Fabulouschrissie on Amazon.com*

50 Intriguing Personal Insights, 2023 edition

In this anthology of real-life stories, twenty-nine writers share fifty fascinating experiences about themselves or those close to them. Take a break from your busy schedule and immerse yourself in this remarkable book. Discover how pivotal moments have affected their lives in unpredictable ways. You will feel stimulated by their honesty and take away a sense of intrigue and fulfilment.

> *"Another great collection. You can read it all in one – or it's perfect for dipping in and out of, a few stories at a time." Julie Haigh, Amazon Top 1,000 reviewer.*

30 Evocative Recollections, 2024 edition

18 authors share the moving experiences that shaped them. From childhood memories to adult revelations, from tragedies to triumphs, these stories will touch your heart, and inspire you to reflect on your own journey.

> *"Tinges of longing, loss, joy, and redemption." Ronald Mackay, Author.*

25 Treasured Memories, 2025 edition

In a world where moments slip away like grains of sand, this anthology celebrates those occasions that linger in our hearts long after they have passed. Let these stories inspire you to cherish your own journey.

> "A trip down memory lane like no other. Stories of yesteryear, when the world was less complicated, combined with humorous and intriguing tales of our human experience. Well worth a read." Elora Canne on Amazon Australia

Follow this link to find all of Jacqueline's books on your local Amazon store: https://author.to/JLambert

About The Author

J acqueline (Jackie) Lambert is an award-winning travel writer, adventure traveller, and dogmother, who loves history and curious facts.

BC (Before Canines) she rafted, rock-climbed, and backpacked around six of the seven continents. A passionate windsurfer and skier, she can fly a plane, has been bitten by a lion, and appeared on Japanese TV as a fire-eater.

AD (After Dog), she quit work in 2016 to hit the road permanently with her husband and four pooches. Initially, they were Adventure Caravanners, who aimed To Boldly Go Where No Van Has Gone Before.

Now, they're at large in a self-converted six-wheel army lorry, with Mongolia in their sights.

All her books and the anthologies that include her travel stories are available on Amazon: https://author.to/JLambert

Mark, Jackie & The Fab Four with The Beast. Photo courtesy of @Liveration, who made a short film about The Beast on YouTube.

Acknowledgements

I would like to thank the following people:

Linn Hart and **Paul Hawkins** of **BolderBooks.com** for the wonderful book cover design.

The 'B' Team – (Really an 'A' Team of Wonderful Beta Readers, many of whom are successful authors) **Judith Benson, Fiona Blundell, Pat Ellis, Chris Evans, Carol Ann Grant Smith, Julie Haigh, Rebecca Hislop, Rebecca Hogue, Don Hughes, Susan Jackson, Drew Johnson, Stephen Malins, Judy Middleton, Chris Moore, Veronica Moore, Valerie Poore, Susan Raymond, Alison Ripley Cubitt, Carrie Riseley, and Lisa Rose Wright** for kindly reading my manuscript and offering their valuable feedback.

My Readers Around the World – as authors, we bare our souls for your entertainment. Your kind words, reviews, and encouragement mean so much.

And of course, **Mark, Kai, Rosie, Ruby** and **Lani** for filling my everyday with unconditional love.

Dog Bless You All!

Printed in Dunstable, United Kingdom